Lyn Marshall has been teaching relaxation and yoga for eighteen years. She works both as a teacher and a therapist using relaxation, yoga and anti-stress techniques, often treating patients referred to her by general practitioners and consultants.

She is considered by many to be one of the experts in her field in Britain, and lectures extensively. Her style of yoga is unique because, although based on the classical postures, it is performed in an unusually slow and gentle way.

Lyn Marshall's three television series, *Wake up to Yoga, Keep up with Yoga* and *Everyday Yoga*, and their accompanying books have proved immensely popular with all ages. She is also the author of *Yoga for Your Children*.

# LYN MARSHALL'S INSTANT STRESS CURE

Immediate Relief from Everyday Stress Problems

To Peter, whose love and support
made this book possible

Text copyright © Lyn Marshall 1988
Photographs copyright © Century Hutchinson 1988

Photographs by Simon Farrell
Cover Photograph by Peter Riding
Design by Dave Goodman

This edition specially produced for
The Leisure Circle Limited
by Century Hutchinson Limited
Brookmount House, 62-65 Chandos Place
London WC2N 4NW

Phototypeset by Tradespools Ltd, Frome
Printed and bound in Great Britain by
Butler and Tanner, Frome

# CONTENTS

# WHAT THIS BOOK IS ABOUT AND WHY IT IS DIFFERENT

Oh! no, you say, not another stress book. There are already so many 'stress' books on the market, so why do we need another? I believe the answer to that question is that there is a very real need for an entirely fresh approach to the subject, one that offers QUICK, INSTANT and EFFECTIVE ways of dealing with our day-to-day stress.

**QUICK** because the 'Stress Cures' in this book take only a few moments of your time to do.

**INSTANT** because you will feel immediate relief from your stress when you carry out the 'Cures'.

**EFFECTIVE** because, quite simply, they work. The 'Cures' are easily learned and virtually anyone can do them, irrespective of age or sex. Most of us are aware of unpleasant and often painful feelings when we are suffering from stress, but few of us actually know what to do to relieve these symptoms and feelings. That means that we have to suffer repeatedly every time we experience stress. We go through life thinking that there is nothing we can do about it.

It is exactly for this reason that I have written this book, because there is a great deal that you can do when stress hits you.

## INSTANT STRESS REMOVAL

It has been my experience that stress sufferers always want quick and easy solutions. They rarely wish to embark on lengthy courses of therapy that may or may not turn out to be successful in the long run. Nor do they wish to incur the heavy financial costs usually associated with such therapies. What they do want is to be able to go to sleep easily and wake refreshed in the morning, without resorting to sleeping pills, and they want to know how to achieve that now, tonight, not in six months' time. The stress sufferer with acute tension pain between the shoulder blades or around the back of the neck needs to know how to relieve it instantly. People who are prone to stress-related headaches, which can strike at any time, may need immediate help before, perhaps, a job interview. Or it may be that restlessness is preventing sleep at night or tension causing a nagging pain during the day, and what the stress sufferer wants to know is how to eliminate it without drugs and how to cure it instantly the next time it happens. Stress can take many forms and there are vast numbers of people suffering from the type of emotional stress that can be caused by such things as shyness and inhibition. This can be crippling and can turn life into a series of ordeals and nightmares, whether the stress is continual or merely occasional. These people simply want to know how to let themselves go so that they can relax and communicate well with the people around them. They, too, want a quick end to their misery, right now, not at some vague point in the future after protracted therapy.

I am not interested in showing you how to 'handle', to 'manage' or to 'live with' your stress, and I am not going to tell you to make dramatic changes to your lifestyle. In the short term at least, most people can't do this and, if you are stressed at the moment, you need help now. My interest is in showing you how to *remove* the harmful effects of stress – whether they be mental, physical or emotional – as instantly as possible, whenever and wherever it hits you.

The simple techniques contained in this self-help manual will make it possible for you to 'cure' yourself without resorting to the use of drugs or conventional therapy. I have been teaching these techniques successfully for eighteen years, and my experience is that even the most stressed individual can learn them quickly and then apply them in his or her life whenever necessary.

## STRESS AND DOCTORS

Stress is responsible for more misery, illness and death than almost anything else in our society. More workdays are lost through stress-related complaints than from the common cold. And it has been estimated that there are literally millions of people who are suffering from the adverse effects of stress today in the Western world and that the figure is rising steadily.

General Practitioners have an ever-increasing caseload of patients with stress-related conditions, but often it seems that they are unable to do much to help. However, it would

be unfair to blame doctors for their ineffectiveness if only because the importance of learning to deal with stress has only recently been included in medical training and, therefore, many older doctors have simply not been taught how to deal with it.

Only thirty years ago the prevailing medical attitude to stress-related complaints tended to be dismissive and even faintly admonishing. It was made clear, for example, to patients suffering from duodenal ulcers, or recurrent backache, that their troubles could be, in a sense, of their own making. Those who suffered from complaints labelled as 'psychosomatic' were often treated unsympathetically and looked on as inadequate personalities, unable to cope with life.

Even though times have changed, and the medical profession now takes stress and its related conditions extremely seriously, doctors still have a problem. While they now appreciate the importance and necessity of relaxation in the removal of stress, they don't have the time (or, indeed, often the knowledge) to show their patients how to achieve it. In many cases, the only treatment that a doctor can offer is drug therapy – the stress, after all, has to be reduced for the welfare of the patient. However, treating stress-related conditions with drugs can, ironically, increase rather than decrease the stress for the following reasons.

It is easy, even over a short period of time, to build up a dependency on drugs that can turn into an addiction. The patient then not only has the original stress problem to deal with, but the problem of the addiction as well. In addition, these drugs can cause many unpleasant side effects that can make the patient feel much worse than before and, at the end of the day, they still won't have learned how to relax. The problem will then simply return and life becomes even more intolerable.

The harmful effect of stress is a heavy burden to carry through life and a totally unnecessary one. I have seen lives virtually transformed overnight by its removal. The aim of this book is to help you to achieve that.

## ARE YOU STRESSED AT THE MOMENT?

It may be that you have bought this book because you are feeling very stressed right now, and you would like to be able to do something to help yourself immediately rather than having to read the book first. This section is for you.

If you have seen your doctor and you have been advised to relax, but you don't know quite where to start, then this section is for you, too.

If you simply want to learn a valuable, key technique that will have an instantly relaxing effect on you, when used in the majority of cases of stress, then this section is also for you.

One of the most common and instantaneous reactions to stress is that we tense our muscles and also restrict our breathing. We often don't know that we are doing this, it just happens. This reaction inevitably leads to us becoming even more stressed, and an upward spiral is then put into effect. There is a particular technique in the book that is designed to counteract this, and you can learn it, practise it and benefit from it immediately.

The technique is called the Out-Breath Technique (*see page 30*). Practise it carefully, following the instructions, and it will relax you and give you a chance to read, select and subsequently practise any other Stress Cures in the book that you feel are appropriate to your stress problems.

If you want to banish stress permanently from your life, it is helpful to understand what stress is and why it is caused and the significance of relaxation in relieving and eliminating it. This information is contained in the following sections called *Understanding Stress* and *Understanding Relaxation*.

# ABOUT THE STRESS CURES

These are divided into three sections: A, B and C. They are planned to be inter-related, so that you can use just one of the Stress Cures on its own, or several of the Stress Cures from all three sections in combination, to deal with the particular physical, mental or emotional problem you have at that time. Using the Stress Cures in this way, your life can literally begin to be stress-free immediately.

## STRESS CURE A: Breathing and Relaxation Techniques

This section shows you how to relax every part of your body and mind at will, using various specific breathing and relaxation techiques.

Many of the techiques in this section can be practised during the day, virtually whenever you find yourself in a stressed situation, and will bring instant relief. The other techniques are for when you have a little more time and privacy and will teach you how to relax completely.

## STRESS CURE B: Stressful Life Situations and their Remedies

This section deals with behavioural problems and contains instant remedies for many common day-to-day problems which can cause stress and anguish.

For example, you may be at a party, your body rigid with tension and fear, with a fixed artificial smile on your face and wishing that you were anywhere but there. There is a particular technique you can use that will instantly relax you and free you to do what you came to do – enjoy yourself (see page 85). Or you may have to address a small group of people at a meeting or give a talk and you are a bundle of nerves at the prospect. There is a technique that will

calm you and take your mind off yourself, thus enabling you to function properly, get your message across, and give the best of yourself (see page 79). You may be on a date and, although you are interested in the person you are with, you are so preoccupied with what he or she is thinking about you that you end up being tense and edgy and certainly not yourself. Once again, there are techniques that will instantly relax you, and that you can use on the spot (see page 83).

Stress Cure B includes other typical behavioural stress problems of the type often experienced in business, social and home life, and teaches you the instant solutions to them.

## STRESS CURE C: Stress-Related Medical and Psychological Problems

This section deals with some of the more common medical and psychological problems that are caused, affected or greatly contributed to by stress, and gives you appropriate tips and advice to either eliminate or considerably ease the conditions. The list contains such complaints as asthma, hypertension, constipation, migraine, panic attacks, nail-biting, indigestion and skin conditions, among many others.

# UNDERSTANDING STRESS

One of the main reasons that stress is such a big problem in our society is the stigma that surrounds it. Actually admitting to being tense and stressed is the hardest obstacle for most people to overcome because there is a feeling that if they are open about being stressed they will be seen to be weak, ineffectual and unable to cope with life.

## ADMITTING THAT YOU HAVE A PROBLEM

There are many very obviously stressed people who go to extreme lengths to hide or deny it. They would rather do anything than admit they are stressed, even to themselves. The irony is that the effort and strain involved in hiding the stress makes it ten times worse, for suppressed stress is self-perpetuating.

To put it another way, driving yourself on, when you are already suffering from the sustained harmful effects of stress, is like continuing to fly a plane that has severe metal fatigue. You may get away with it for a few more flights but you could be heading for disaster.

There is a chain reaction with stress and the longer you allow it to persist the more dangerous it can become. In this situation complete mental breakdown, necessitating protracted therapy, is a very real possibility. It is important therefore to be honest with yourself and admit that you do have a stress problem, because the earlier you deal with it, the less damage it can do to you.

The lists on the following pages have been designed to enable you to identify how your stress manifests itself in your life and your health.

## PERSONAL STRESS CHECKLIST – IS THIS YOU?

Check through the lists, noting on a piece of paper the symptoms that apply to you, bearing in mind that you may have to note several items from different groups. This is because stress seldom affects just one aspect of you or your life, and it is more often the case that you will be physically, mentally and emotionally affected.

By making your own list in this way, you are acknowledging which of the negative stress signs apply specifically to you. This will then enable you to see clearly which symptoms and reactions you wish to eliminate from your life.

It is quite possible that there will be many items that apply to you, and your list may look frighteningly long. Don't worry about this, because you may well find that many of the symptoms and reactions will disappear simultaneously when you begin to apply the appropriate Stress Cure. However, make any problem or problems that are severely affecting your life your priority. Later on, you can deal with the less important ones.

The following are some of the more common physical, mental and emotional signs of stress.

## PHYSICAL STRESS SIGNS

Tension and pain in: Neck/Shoulders/Back.
Tension in any other specific area of your body – state where.
Pain – intermittent or recurring – in any of the following:

Head
Face
Neck
Arms
Hands
Stomach
Buttocks
Legs
Feet and toes

Shortness of breath
Unnecessary sweating
Raised blood pressure
Eyestrain
Headaches, intermittent or recurring
Migraine
Constipation
Indigestion
Hypertension
Asthma
Hyperventilation
Upset stomach
Excessive fatigue
Flatulence

Pre-Menstrual Tension
Dysmenorrhoea
Nausea
Insomnia
Allergies
Skin conditions.

## Eating Problems

Loss of appetite – intermittent or recurring.
Increased appetite – intermittent or recurring.
Anorexia nervosa – fear of weight-gain leading to extremely restricted diet and possible emaciation.
Bulimia nervosa – obsessive and compulsive eating often accompanied by self-induced vomiting and the use of purgatives.
Becoming excessively finicky about particular foods or foods prepared in a special way.
Having an illogical aversion to certain foods.

## Drinking Problems

Increased consumption of alcohol.
Dependence on alcohol.
Fear of alcohol.
Excessive consumption of any liquids including coffee, tea, colas and other soft drinks, or even water.
An aversion to, dislike or fear of, drinking any liquid.

## Habitual Mannerisms

Nail-biting.
Picking at the fingers.
Touching the face constantly.
Touching and checking the hair constantly.
Scratching the nose or face repeatedly.
Stuttering.
Licking the lips frequently.

Biting the lips.
Swallowing repeatedly.
Coughing unnecessarily.
Blinking repeatedly.
Hunching the shoulders.
Drumming the fingers.
Tapping the feet.
Picking fluff off one's clothes endlessly.
Needing to talk incessantly.

## MENTAL AND EMOTIONAL STRESS SYMPTOMS

Depression.
Anxiety.
Nervousness.
Fear.
Anger.
Embarrassment.
Dissatisfaction.
Lack of confidence.
Low self-image.
Fear of inadequacy.
Irritability.
Aggressiveness.
Self-absorption.
Being hypercritical of yourself and others.
Being hyperactive.
Having suicidal thoughts when you feel you've
simply had enough.
Panic attacks.
Phobias.

**Note:** *It is possible that some of the above
conditions could be attributed to poor physical
health, with stress not necessarily being a
contributory factor. If you are in any doubt, I
would most strongly urge you to clarify the
situation by consulting your doctor.*

## GOOD AND BAD STRESS

One of the first things I want to make quite clear
is that all stress is not bad, even though most of
us use the word in a negative way. Stress in
fact is necessary to maintain life. It acts as a
trigger enabling the body to rise to all sorts of
challenges and is the spur needed for
achievement. It is stress that powers the mother's
sprint against oncoming traffic to rescue a child
who has strayed on to the road; stress that
impels the jockey to be first at the winning-post
and stress that enables the driver to make an
emergency stop.

Another example of the positive side of stress
is when you have an awful lot to do and very
little time to do it in. Somehow you quicken
things up and it all gets done.

Stress can therefore play a beneficial role in
our lives but it can also play a bad and
detrimental one. When scientists use the word
'stress', they mean the body's general response
to any demands made upon it. Quite literally, it
is whenever the body is put into a state of
arousal. This arousal state can be triggered by
virtually anything, good or bad, including the
things, people and events going on around us
all the time in our daily lives. It can be stimulated
by alarm, excitement, worry, sorrow, or even
joy. The interesting thing is that the same
physiological process takes place in the body
no matter whether the stress has been caused
by something pleasant (like winning the pools)
or something unpleasant (like getting the sack).

The degree of arousal or stress that is
experienced for exactly the same life event will
vary considerably from person to person, as
does the way that the stress is handled. This is,
in fact, the key issue in determining whether
stress is potentially good or bad for us.

Stress is acceptable, harmless and may even
be desirable when we don't suppress or hide
our feelings about it, or when we can diffuse or
relieve the stress by relaxing and letting go.

On the other hand, stress is potentially dangerous when we hide or deny it.

Research has established that an individual's ability to withstand unrelieved stress has a limit. Prolonged stress causes a build-up of physical and mental strain and tension that has the power to cause real damage. The extent of this damage can be seen by the extreme conditions listed on the *Personal Stress Checklist* (*see page 10*). This book is dedicated to reducing or eliminating the 'bad' effects of stress.

## STRESS AND HOW IT AFFECTS THE BODY

A quick, natural and truly remarkable process takes place in the body in certain circumstances. For example, if we are challenged by an imminent exam, a rumour at work of redundancies or a violent quarrel with a partner. What happens is that, automatically, our bodies go into overdrive and there is a dramatic change throughout the entire organism.

First, the stress factor, whatever it might be that has alerted us, excites a small organ in the base of the brain, causing it to produce a substance that stimulates the pituitary gland to release certain hormones into the bloodstream. These hormones in turn induce the adrenal glands to secrete the adrenalin, noradrenalin and cortisone that are needed to prepare the body for the emergency or challenge facing it. Among other changes that take place, sugar production is increased to aid in the repair of damaged tissue; the heart rate increases and accordingly the blood pressure rises. The muscles harden and tense in readiness for action. The process of digestion stops and acid secretion is increased in the stomach. Breathing quickens up as the lungs try to take in more oxygen and the body temperature rises significantly. Our nerves are highly charged and our reflexes sharpened.

This process puts the body in a state of readiness to meet the challenge, and it can literally save our lives in an emergency. It charges us up in preparation for imminent danger so that we can instantly react by either resisting or running away. It is what is commonly known as the 'fight or flight' response.

Our forefathers needed this instant response in order to cope with the many physically life-threatening situations of their existence. Today, despite endless reports of violent crime, few of us actually experience such physically dangerous encounters but we nevertheless feel that we are in danger of a different sort. Our fear is less for our physical and more for our mental and emotional survival. When we feel that our self-image or ego is likely to be attacked, we feel just as threatened as did our forefathers many years ago, and we are gripped by just as real a fear.

Our physiological reactions to stress are probably the same as those of primitive man, who had constantly to watch out for his physical survival. I suspect he recovered from the effects of stress, once the danger had passed, far more quickly than we do. We tend to hang on to our stress for very prolonged periods, resulting in extreme physical, mental and emotional damage.

It also seems probable that our ancestors felt no shame in spontaneously displaying the signs of their stress and tension, whereas we feel self-conscious if someone notices if our hands are shaking, our teeth are clenched or our cheeks are red with embarrassment. Indeed our ancestors probably turned such symptoms of stress to their advantage. For example, fear can often make the hair on our bodies stand on end. It has been suggested that they needed and used this physical reaction to danger to give the illusion to the enemy – just as cats fluff themselves up before a fight – that the body was larger than it actually was, and therefore a more frightening prospect. The bigger and more powerful one was, the better the chance of victory.

Our inhibitions and efforts to hide our physical reactions and feelings only serve to trap the stress and tension inside us and make it much worse.

## WHY IS STRESS PHYSICALLY BAD FOR YOU?

If the body is repeatedly put into a stressed state or kept that way for prolonged periods of time, it can lead not only to the many conditions listed in *Stress Cure C*, but to some that are even more serious and sometimes fatal. The consequence of sustained stress is that eventually the body's reserves of energy are so severely depleted that the sufferer cannot recover.

One of the many reasons why stress can be so damaging is the spiralling effect that it can have, and this is what can cause a relatively minor complaint to develop into a much more dangerous one. When you become stressed and are unable to relieve the stress, various symptoms begin to appear. They may start as extremely trivial things having little more than a nuisance value, but if they are ignored they can turn into the sort of painful and unpleasant conditions that demand your time and attention.

If the stress is allowed to persist unrelieved, some even more severe conditions may develop. For example, if the heart rate and blood pressure are continually being raised, and maintained that way for prolonged periods, as happens when we are under stress, the blood is more likely to clot, and the arteries to harden. Strokes, angina and heart attacks can result.

Stress can also have a detrimental effect on the immune system, rendering it less effective against disease. It is now known that continual stress prevents the body from fulfilling its normal function of repairing, regenerating and

subsequently protecting itself. The energy needed for this vital process of restoring the body's stability is used up instead by the stress.

Acid secretion in the stomach increases with stress but digestion stops, so the acid cannot do its proper job. Irritation of the stomach lining can follow, leading to gastric or duodenal ulcers.

Added to these there is the considerable danger of serious side effects of stress manifesting themselves in alcoholism, drug addiction and severe depression. These all have the power to affect your life drastically and wreck your prospects for a healthy and happy future.

It is clear that sustained stress must be regarded as highly dangerous, possibly life threatening, and should be treated accordingly.

## HOW STRESS AFFECTS OUR EMOTIONS

For most of us the experience of being under stress is in itself a very bad feeling. That may seem a simplistic way of looking at stress but I think it is helpful. When you are suffering from physical, mental or emotional stress, or all three, your feelings may be painful, disturbing, anxious and so on, as you try to carry on normally with your life. Your workload may seem heavy, your colleagues and family irritating, and that phone bill that plops onto the mat the last straw. Underlying all these unpleasant feelings relating to the outside world is another, overwhelmingly strong emotion. This concerns you, and how you actually feel about yourself.

When we are stressed, our self-image, our ability to perform and therefore our confidence, are all affected, and this makes us very self-critical. We begin to worry about our standing with the people around us, and resolve to do better to prove to both them and ourselves that we 'can do it'. This is a very strong motivating force and it drives us on, creating ever more pressure. This, of course, is happening at precisely the time when we should, so far as our health is concerned, be doing the opposite, namely letting up, calming down and relaxing. But we are talking here about a feeling so powerful that it can cause the kind of serious symptoms and conditions listed on the previous pages, all of which, as we have seen, have a highly detrimental effect.

It is possible, however, to take control of this driving force, to turn the tables and learn how to quieten these strong negative feelings about ourselves. As this process takes place, self-esteem and confidence will rise, and this in turn will eliminate feelings of self-doubt and inadequacy. The need to push constantly for-wards to prove yourself will diminish, and you will discover that there isn't so much to be self-critical about anymore.

As time goes on, you will find that the bad and powerful feeling that comes with stress will gradually get weaker and weaker until it just ceases to exist at all.

## STRESS AND HOW IT AFFECTS THE WHOLE OF YOU

The 'whole' person is involved when stress is present, and that means that although the stress may start in the mind it inevitably manifests itself in the emotions and in the body as well. I shall illustrate this point by taking, as an example, what is commonly referred to as a 'panic attack'.

This sort of attack is extremely common and experienced by thousands of people every day. However, that doesn't alter the fact that it can be and often is a truly terrifying experience. The reasons for panic attacks are many, and you will find advice on how to understand this sort of attack and the practical steps you can take to deal with it in the *Stress Cure C* section (*page 104). See also Hyperventilation (page 112)* in the same section.

Panic attacks do vary according to the individual's situation and circumstances, but the following is what happens in most cases.

The panic usually begins with the person feeling an acute stab of fear, stemming generally from some form of self-doubt. That fear causes the person to stop suddenly and freeze up. Everything is tensed. The muscles are gripped tightly. The lungs and diaphragm can't expand to take in enough air. The person feels that the breathing is restricted and that increases the panic. The tension builds up and the breathing becomes even more shallow causing the person to think that he or she literally can't breathe. Images of being about to die follow, of being out of control and unable to do anything about it. The breath then comes in gasps. The heart rate increases. The chest and throat area feel hot, tight and heavy. The temperature goes up and the hands feel clammy with sweat. Swallowing is difficult and it often feels like an imminent heart attack. This of course increases the panic still further and can sometimes even lead to total unconsciousness.

This may seem like an extreme example, and perhaps it is, but it serves to illustrate how stress can affect the whole of you. The stress may well have started in the mind, but it also had an alarming and immediate effect on both the emotions and the body.

Even in more mild examples of stress, you can be sure that every aspect of you is being affected in a detrimental way.

## SELF-CONSCIOUSNESS AND SELF-AWARENESS

It often seems that stress is something that is happening to us without our playing any part in it at all. It has been described to me many times as an external force over which we have no power. But the truth of the matter is that we do have both the power and the means to control ourselves and our reactions. It is true that there are situations that are inevitably stressful – such as driving on a busy motorway or watching someone you love in pain – but in most of the situations that we encounter in everyday life it is we who are exerting, increasing and sustaining our stress, not some outside influence or event. Many of us are simply not aware that we are doing this. Learning how to recognize the stress signs in yourself by observing your reactions and your behaviour, becoming, in effect, self-aware, is therefore very important, because you can then take immediate steps to counteract and disperse them.

It is essential, however, to differentiate clearly between self-awareness and self-consciousness because they are not one and the same thing.

## Self-consciousness

Self-consciousness can be a liability that one should try to eliminate as far as possible, since it can often be a very stressful and painful experience, with the person becoming obsessed with how they appear to others. In its extreme form, self-consciousness can so severely affect the sufferers' lives that they actually avoid contact with people. This problem and how to cope with it is referred to later (*see page 99*).

**Clothes** I would like to offer a quick word of advice on the subject of clothes to anyone who suffers from self-consciousness. This is not as frivolous as it may seem, because the type of clothes you wear can actually increase or decrease your stress. Avoid wearing clothes that need constant attention, or you may find that you want to keep fiddling with them. It is better to wear really comfortable clothes, even if they have to be special for your work. In particular, don't wear anything too tight round the waist. You need to be able to breathe deeply in order to relax and, as you will see when you come to the breathing techniques,

that means your waist area has to be able to expand as you breathe in and out. The neck and throat also need to feel free, so try not to wear anything tight or restrictive in that area either. After you have dressed in the morning, check yourself thoroughly in the mirror and satisfy yourself that you look all right. After that, try to resist the urge to think about your clothes and how you look.

There is a particular technique explained later that will teach you how to divert your attention from yourself. It is called the Deviation of Focus Technique (*see page 34*). If you are self-conscious, it really is worthwhile to study and practise this, because being continually worried about one's appearance can cause additional stress.

## Self-awareness

Unlike self-consciousness, which is a negative feeling, self-awareness is a positive state of mind. It enables us to take an objective view of ourselves for the purpose of confirming that all is well. It allows us to do a body check if we are stressed, and then to take immediate steps to remove that stress. We are then able to let go of ourselves and appreciate fully the experience of the moment, our attention no longer being focused on our stress and strain. Self-awareness used in this way is remarkably liberating.

One of the most common signs of stress is that we hunch our shoulders. This may be an unconscious desire to sink into ourselves for self-protection. We grip the stomach or buttock muscles out of nervousness, assuring ourselves that as these parts of us aren't visible, nobody will notice. We may constantly transfer our body weight from one foot to the other, or slouch down, trying to appear smaller. Other stress signs are breathlessness, repeatedly scratching the nose or ear, or constantly clearing the throat or licking the lips, and so on.

By becoming more self-aware you will recognize that it is actually you who is causing your stress and it is therefore also you who can eliminate it. This is how you go about it.

The first thing you do is to check your stance. It is amazing how much difference a change in your body position can make to your sense of security. Start by adjusting your feet so that they are both planted squarely on the ground about ten inches apart with your weight evenly distributed. Then check that the muscles in the calves, thighs and buttocks are relaxed enough for you not to be aware of them. This not only improves your sense of being solid on the ground, but also conveys a message to the person you are with that you are confident. This change of stance also improves your balance.

Then drop your shoulders and feel the muscular release, not only in the shoulders themselves but also in the neck and top of the back. Check your arm and hand positions and, where possible, let them hang loosely at your sides. You are then ready to change your breathing so that you not only allow yourself to relax and to breathe more deeply, but also to release any remaining gripped muscles, including the stomach.

All these minor adjustments are totally unnoticeable to anyone but you. They relax your physical stance, and they also loosen up your emotional attitude, giving you a really positive sense that you have *a right to be there in that situation*. You can then simply experience the situation for what it is and not your own discomfort.

This is just one common example, but the techniques will work in any 'stress' situation. The physical, mental and emotional checks will become second nature until you literally don't need to do them any more. (See also *The Body Check, page 66*).

## SELF-VALUATION

The way we value ourselves as human beings is one of the greatest causes of stress. Our self-image is formed by a number of factors throughout childhood and adolescence but is invariably influenced by comparing ourselves with other people. We live in a society where outward signs of achievement are extremely important and so there is unremitting pressure to do constantly better, in order to compete. A certain amount of competition is good and healthy, but when the need to achieve and to be seen to be achieving becomes a really powerful driving force in one's life, then severe stress and ill-health are often the result.

I believe that we can change the basis of our criterion for self-valuation in several ways, and that by doing so we can remove stress.

Firstly, learning how to be quietly alone with yourself, not doing anything, not making any demands, just simply being, is a very valuable step towards really getting to know and value yourself. Just being still and quiet, even if it is only for a few minutes a day, to concentrate on yourself and your feelings, is a luxury that we can all afford no matter how busy we are. This doesn't entail anything complicated at all, and is not a specific form of meditation. By using the simple breathing and relaxation techniques explained in the *Stress Cure A* section, in privacy and quiet – even for just five to ten minutes a day – you will quickly begin to know yourself. You will become more comfortable with yourself, and finally be able to accept, approve and love yourself.

This time spent alone, doing nothing, is a very alien concept in our society. We are not used to stopping and simply reflecting and feeling, and you may feel a sense of guilt that you should be out there doing and achieving. However, don't let this deter you because after even a few days of this private time you will have begun to feel the benefit. Try to take your private break from life at the same time each day. That way it quickly becomes part of your everyday routine.

## Accept Yourself as You Are

Another way to change your self-valuation is to try gradually to stop comparing yourself with others quite so much, and to think of yourself as being unique, which of course you are. You can't make yourself better-looking, brighter, more dynamic, more sophisticated or whatever, by sheer effort, any more than you can make yourself taller or shorter. By trying to, you will only create stress and self-dissatisfaction. Often, when we do begin to accept ourselves more for what we are, and stop constantly comparing ourselves with others, we liberate ourselves in a way that allows natural growth and development to take place.

Another common fault when we are assessing our value is to tell ourselves that we will be more valuable when we have become materially richer, or have greater recognition and respect from our peers, or when somebody loves us, and so on. In other words we assume that self-value is always going to rise tomorrow, when that other thing happens. You have to accept yourself today, as you are, or you will never be good enough in your own eyes. Try to accept the fact that you are a remarkable and individual being and celebrate your differences from others rather than trying to be like them.

We have, after all, only one life, and to use so much of it worrying, striving and aspiring to be someone or something else seems to me to be downright foolish. So try to love and appreciate what you are.

## HOW TO SAY 'NO'

'No' is one of the most powerful words in the English language. It leaves absolutely no room for doubt, but many people find themselves desperately hunting around for an alternative reponse, especially in reply to an invitation or a request. Saying 'no' when you are not used to saying it can be a frightening prospect, but why?

Well, for a start, we think it's rude. It sounds abrupt to our own ears and dismissive of the other person. We tell ourselves that we don't want to hurt the other person's feelings. So in answer to the invitation to come round for dinner, we say: 'Oh!, I'd love to but I can't because. . . .' The excuse sounds weak and our self-respect diminishes. Nobody feels good about lying so why do we do it?

I believe that we make these feeble excuses not solely because we are afraid of hurting the other person's feelings, but also out of a fear of adversely affecting our own popularity. The sense of self-worth for many people is gauged by how popular they think they are, so the desire to be 'nice' about refusing invitations or to be always obliging when asked to do things at work and so on is very strong. But trying to be 'nice', far from getting you what you want, can often create tremendous stress.

If we say 'yes' when we really mean 'no', a powerful resentment builds up in us, not only towards the person we are dealing with, but against ourselves for not having the strength and courage to say 'no'.

Many stressed people that I have dealt with were stressed because they had put themselves under pressure by accepting something that they would much rather have refused. They had spent a large part of their lives both at work and at home doing things that in all honesty they either hadn't wanted or didn't feel that they were obliged to do. As soon as they began to be a bit more assertive, and to respond honestly by saying 'no', the pressure immediately lifted.

Being assertive, if it doesn't come naturally to you – and it doesn't to most people – is a skill that can be learned. If you find it difficult to say 'no' when it is really appropriate to do so, you are probably creating stress for yourself and living under considerable strain. How to learn to be more self-assertive is explained later (*see page 97*).

## SUCCESS AND FAILURE

The need to succeed in our society is paramount, but what is success?

Is it working so hard that it becomes your whole life?

Is it being so ambitious that 'getting there' is all that matters?

Is it acquiring the visible trappings of success?

Is it being the same as, or better than, everyone around you?

We are seduced into believing that success, money and advancement will assure us happiness, but do they? Very often they bring the reverse by creating stress, discontent and great unhappiness.

My definition of true success is when individuals have decided how they truly want to spend their lives in order to have maximum contentment and satisfaction – and subsequently carry it through, with or without the approval of society.

It is true that there are people who appear to thrive on hard work and pressure, and there is nothing wrong with that if it provides a way of life which brings genuine and lasting satisfaction. However, we all react differently, and it is often the case that people force themselves to live a high-pressure existence out of fear that they might appear to be failures if they don't.

Fear is one of the most potent causes of stress, and fear of failure is not only terrible to live with but, ironically, it sabotages chances of succeeding by undermining our ability to perform.

If you are stressed, you may need to rethink just what success and failure really mean to

you, and what is and isn't valuable. It may then involve letting go of many of the preconceived ideas of how you should live your life.

I have found it helps someone in this situation to make two lists. The first, listing all the things and activities in the person's life, including work, that are pleasurable and nice, no matter how trivial, and the second, containing all the things that are unpleasant. The effect of seeing your likes and dislikes in writing actually forces you to acknowledge them; your lists may well contain some surprises when you see what you do and don't really enjoy. In this way, the lists will give you an opportunity for self-examination.

I am not suggesting that you will be able to eliminate everything unpleasant from your second list, but you will be able to use the lists as a guide and gradually work towards making your priorities in life the things that truly give you pleasure and satisfaction. Likewise, you can begin to cut down and in some cases eliminate the things that don't. Obviously, we all have to do many things in life that we don't like, and I'm not suggesting that we all down tools and leap off to a desert island. Many of us, however, could stop doing the things that we think we ought to do, but don't really have to do, and thereby dramatically reduce the stress in our lives.

## IS STRESS CONTAGIOUS?

The answer to that question is often 'yes', but that needn't be the case.

We have all experienced situations where we have started out relaxed and calm but the atmosphere around us has become charged up and tense. We get sucked into it, with the result that we ourselves become unnecessarily stressed, drained and exhausted.

People often think that they are helpless in this kind of situation, but this is not so. It is you who ultimately chooses whether or not you are going to allow yourself to get caught up in other people's stress. It is also you who can decide not to get caught up in it.

In the *Stress Cure B* section you will discover how you can control your own reactions in all sorts of common situations, no matter how stressed the people that you are with. There are simple techniques that will enable you to take instant control of yourself irrespective of what is going on around you. You may then subsequently find that not only do you calm yourself down but your calmness has a strong influence on the person or people around you.

The cost of stress is high in terms of the huge amounts of energy that are used up, plus the resultant wear and tear on your whole system. So why pay for other people's stress when you have the ability to avoid it? It is enough of a burden to have to deal with your own. Stress may indeed be contagious but you can protect yourself against it by being aware of what to do as soon as you encounter it.

## WHAT IS A STRESS-FREE LIFE?

This book is all about eliminating harmful stress from your life, so what will life be like when you have succeeded in doing this?

Will it be bland, dull and uninteresting?

Will it put an end to the highs and lows of life?

Will you be in a state of apathy most of the time, not getting worked up about anything very much?

Will it curtail your excitement in any way? The answer to these and many other similar questions is of course 'no'.

There is nothing bland or boring about saying goodbye to a multitude of unpleasant symptoms and feelings. About being able to sleep better, work and play better. About having surplus energy, no matter what your age, to spend where and when it matters most.

Highs and lows are a natural part of life, and we couldn't have one without the other. Being

on a continual 'high' would, in any case, be exhausting and dangerous. Living a more stress-free life, however, does mean that there are more high points and less low ones, and it also means that if and when the depressions come, you can help to prevent them from becoming deep and intense.

Eliminating your stress doesn't mean that you will feel detached and stop caring about the important things in life, but it does mean that you won't get steamed up about the many unimportant ones, as so often happens when we are stressed.

You will find yourself much more open to new ideas and willing to take on different and exciting challenges. You will gain a sense of freedom that allows you to discover and taste new experiences. Life will once again become the exciting adventure that it was when you were a child.

## Will I Grind to a Halt?

Many people seem to think of themselves as a kind of motoring force and are often afraid that if they slow down or stop the motor will cut out and they won't be able to restart it. They fear that they will totally lose their grip and their ability to handle their lives. In other words, they feel that their stress is actually propelling them, and that without it they wouldn't be able to function and would grind to a halt.

In reality, that doesn't happen. What does happen is that as each stress is removed the considerable time and attention that you previously devoted to that stress, its causes and manifestations, are given back to you. As a result, you have more time and energy to devote to the important and enjoyable things in your life, and more emotional reserves to appreciate them.

When you are stressed, in contrast, any spare time you have is often what I call 'poor quality time'. You may be spending your leisure hours on things that are considered relaxing and enjoyable or with the people closest to you, but the influence of the stress is such that your thoughts and feelings keep coming back to *you*, preventing you from enjoying and getting the most out of the current moment. In other words, you are not able to truly appreciate the things and the people that you care about most. Life under stress is considerably diminished because the stress occupies so much of your time and attention. By eliminating the effects of stress as much as you can, your experience of life is expanded and greatly enhanced.

Being able to live a totally stress-free existence is a wonderful goal, and I hope that by using this book you can begin to work towards it. However, if you are suffering from a lot of different stresses, it may be more realistic to try and cut out the stress bit by bit, because aiming to eliminate it all at once can actually create more stress. Using the Cures, start with the most urgent problems in your life and then gradually move on to the others. As you succeed, your confidence will grow enormously with the proof that it is you who has the power to control and get rid of your stress. Your knowledge of your own ability to 'cure' yourself will then continue to spur you on.

# UNDERSTANDING RELAXATION

## WHY IS IT SO DIFFICULT TO RELAX?

The short answer is that relaxation is a skill that we simply haven't been taught.

While we were growing up, most of us were never either encouraged or permitted to let go and simply do nothing. When and if we did, we were usually admonished. Relaxation wasn't regarded as important, necessary or desirable.

On the contrary, we were constantly being urged to be 'active', and if we weren't we were regarded as lazy. No one wants to be accused of being lazy so we were motivated from childhood to fill up our time with so-called 'worthwhile' activities.

In some countries and cultures, relaxation and doing nothing is built into the way of life, sometimes because the climate makes this a necessity. For example, in Latin countries they have their siestas – time off every day specifically to relax. In the East, being still and contemplative is considered admirable. In our Western society, however, doing nothing is usually criticized and condemned. We therefore feel guilty if we are not putting our physical and mental energies towards a definite end. Most people, after all, want to be seen as 'qualifying'

members of society, worthy of respect and approval.

This is a very strong motivating force and is why most people find it so difficult to relax. Guilt about 'letting go' affects most of us very strongly. So much so that, when we get off the treadmill to relax, even for short periods, we often feel bad about ourselves – indeed, this form of guilt is so ingrained that we can even feel guilty when we are alone and no one else can see us relaxing.

Most people feel entitled to allow themselves to relax only at very specific and limited times and to do so outside these times can seem almost like a crime to them. This way of allocating relaxation time might actually work, but it is often the case that people are so hyped up and stressed that when they have their 'permissible' relaxation breaks, they find that they are unable to relax.

The question that I am most commonly asked is: 'How can I relax? I've tried so hard, but nothing seems to work.' The answer is that, like many other things in life, relaxation is easy when you know how. People often think that you can 'make' yourself relax, but you can't. Making yourself relax implies an effort, which in itself creates tension. You have to 'allow' yourself to relax, and this is the subtle but very important distinction.

We often think that we are relaxed when we aren't, and there are many situations that illustrate this. Watch people, for example, when they are sitting and supposedly relaxing. You will see them in awkward positions, often fidgeting, and gripping and using muscles unnecessarily. This also applies to most of us as we go through the motions of everyday living. We are constantly using muscles that are totally unnecessary for the activity in hand, and thereby not only tiring ourselves, but also creating stress.

In recent times the serious consequences of stress have come to be widely recognized, making people much more aware of the absolute necessity for relaxation. I believe that it is such an important life skill that it should be taught in schools. I certainly think that, with today's pressures, everybody needs to learn how to relax.

Although in the past it may have seemed very difficult for you to relax, you will find that the simple relaxation techniques explained in the *Stress Cure A* section will quickly teach you how. That means that you will be able to relax your whole body, or specific parts of it, when tension is present. There are techniques that will teach you how to recognize unconscious stress and show you how to deal with it, and there are also techniques for clearing your mind at will.

## WHY IS IT SO IMPORTANT TO RELAX?

Think of your body as a machine. Superbly constructed though that machine is, as with all machines, if you don't periodically turn it off, it will simply wear itself out.

As human machines our body design is nothing short of miraculous and, because it is so good, we are able to take a certain number of liberties and risks with it. However, built in to the design is also the absolute need to counteract activity with rest and relaxation. This is a natural part of our life and our body rhythm, and it means that there are times of high and low energy, both physical and mental. If we ignore that rhythm and deprive ourselves of rest when we need it, we throw the body into chaos and it becomes stressed. That is when things can start to go seriously wrong with our health.

There are very specific tasks that our bodies have to perform when we are resting so that we can continue to function at optimum level. If we constantly ignore the messages that our bodies are sending us to relax, these tasks cannot be performed efficiently. That means that the body's own ability to heal, protect and regenerate itself can become severely impaired.

The natural order of things is for us to work our bodies and our minds, and then rest and relax. In this respect I think that we have a lot to learn from the animal kingdom. Animals don't have any qualms about relaxing. When they have exerted themselves, they simply lie down and recuperate. Our lives, of course, are structured in a very much more formal way, and even though many of us would like to emulate the animals and collapse in a heap when we have had enough, we obviously can't allow ourselves to do this. What we can do, however, is to become much more conscious and tuned in to ourselves, so that when we really need to relax we react by trying, as far as possible, to indulge ourselves in that relaxation without any recriminations. It is, after all, using our time in the most valuable way. We can't trade in our bodies when they become damaged or worn out. Surely then, the priority in our lives must be to take good care of them.

The mind, like the body, needs adequate time off to rest, otherwise it can simply get over-loaded. The human brain is capable of storing an amazing amount of information and calling it up as soon as it is needed. It has extraordinary powers and abilities but, again like the body, if it doesn't get adequate rest, it begins to function inefficiently. Concentration and memory deteriorate, and it becomes harder to perform even simple, everyday tasks. This can have a spiralling effect. You blame yourself for your inability to perform well, resolve to try even harder thereby creating more stress and pressure, and subsequently function even worse than before. The harder you try the more stressed and worn out you become. There really are no *ifs* and *buts* here; if you wish to live a healthy, stress-free life, it is of the utmost importance to allow your mind to relax and unwind regularly. This you can learn to do by using the 'stress cures' described later.

I have found that the following technique is very valuable in helping stressed people to relax their minds, and you may like to try it.

## THE DAYDREAM TECHNIQUE

I was a child much given to daydreams at school, and I can clearly remember being constantly rebuked for 'not concentrating' on my work. So I grew up to think, like many of us, that daydreaming was wrong, and, when I began to drift off into some fantasy or other, I swiftly shook myself out of it.

Over the years, my opinion of daydreams has changed. They can be a wonderful form of mental relaxation, if used correctly, and a kind of safety valve where stress is concerned. They can give your brain time out to ease the pressures of the day and there is nothing wrong in allowing yourself to daydream for a few minutes, even two or three times a day. Just let your mind wander wherever it will, and think pleasant thoughts. It may be a memory of a past holiday, or of moments spent with someone special, or it may be purely imaginary. Virtually anything that comes to mind that is pleasurable.

Just let yourself drift with it for a few moments and then gently bring yourself back to reality and continue with your normal life. This temporary break in your routine won't impair your efficiency but it will bring you some instant mental relaxation and renewed energy. So go ahead and enjoy it. Daydreaming will do you good. A word of caution, however. There is a time and place for everything and it would obviously be highly irresponsible to daydream in situations where you would be endangering either yourself or those around you as, for instance, whilst driving.

## SLEEP

We have talked about the general importance of relaxation during one's waking hours, but how about sleeping? Surely this is the one time when everybody should be able to let go and relax completely. However, going to bed at night is often not the relaxing experience it ought to be, as the statistics for sleeping pill prescriptions prove, but why is this?

It is due partly to the fact that many people don't know that there are good and bad body positions for sleeping, and that a faulty sleeping position can actually put the body under severe strain even though it is supposed to be resting. The correct position *(see page 43)* is one in which every muscle is able to relax, and where the breathing apparatus is totally unrestricted.

Another reason why sleep is not the relaxing experience it ought to be is the fact that many people simply can't switch off their minds. Thoughts keep swimming round and round in their heads whilst they periodically glance at the clock, noting with horror how little sleep they will have had before they have to get up again. Eventually they fall into an exhausted doze that is too short and of poor quality, and spend the next day shattered and not able to function properly.

Sound sleep is essential for a healthy mind and body, and it is possible for everyone to achieve it. It does mean learning about relaxation and practising the correct breathing, relaxing and visualising techniques, but the success rate is high and so are the rewards: namely, a really good night's sleep from which you awake refreshed and regenerated.

# BREATHING – THE KEY

Breathing is such a significant part of relaxation that its importance cannot be over emphasized. It is, without doubt, the real key to relaxation.

People often think that because we breathe naturally and automatically from birth we don't need to learn anything more about it. If you are a stress sufferer, however, you do, for several reasons.

One of the common effects of stress is that your breathing becomes affected. As tension builds up, your breathing becomes more shallow and rapid and it can sometimes seem difficult to take in enough air. Your mind tells you to breathe more deeply but your body tension prevents it. Therefore, one of the first steps towards relaxation is to learn how to stop that chain reaction. This, and all the other techniques mentioned in this chapter, are explained in detail in the *Stress Cure A* section.

## What is Deep Breathing?

It is very important to get fixed in your mind the fact that tension simply cannot co-exist with *correct*, relaxed, deep breathing; the one totally cancels out the other. It is, however, vital that you learn to breathe in the right way.

We often think that we are taking a deep breath when we aren't. Many people, knowing that deep breathing is supposed to calm them down when stressed, will take a huge gulp of air, assuming that this will control their breathing and consequently enable them to relax. Well, although it is true that deep and controlled breathing will calm you, a rapid, energetic in-breath of this type actually has the reverse effect. It will increase rather than decrease your tension and stress because, as you breathe in like this, you automatically tense your neck and shoulders, and in fact this type of breathing is shallow rather than deep.

It is often assumed that the chest has to expand in order to take a good, deep breath, but in fact you should first allow the diaphragm (the area just below the rib cage) to expand, followed by the chest, with the majority of movement being in the diaphragm area. We actually do breathe this way when we are not aware of it. If, for example, you look at somebody who is sleeping on their back, you will see how the diaphragm rises and falls, as they breathe in and out – but you will see hardly any movement in the chest itself. Test this for yourself. Lie down, place your fingertips gently on the diaphragm, palms downward, and let your elbows rest beside you. Then gently relax your arms and hands. As you breathe in, you will feel your hands move apart as the diaphragm expands and then move together again as it contracts.

This method of breathing should, where possible, be implemented into our normal, everyday lives if we want to relax – and that means learning to become very aware of how we actually breathe so that we can correct it when necessary.

## The Out-Breath Technique

We always tend to think that the in-breath is the influential factor in controlling the speed of our breathing, but in fact it is the out-breath that we have to concentrate on much more. The way to breathe correctly when you want to release tension is to concentrate *purely* on the out-breath. The in-breath will always take care of itself and you will automatically take in sufficient air and oxygen without thinking about it, even though it may seem that you are taking in very little breath at the time. When you learn to execute this technique *(see page 30)* you will see how, as you breathe out *gently* and *slowly*, the tension will leave you along with the breath and you will feel an instant sensation of relief and letting go. After several more breaths, you will feel calm and relaxed. In terms of the fight against stress, this way of breathing is one of the most effective techniques I know.

There are many areas of your life where a change in your method of breathing will greatly help you: for example, simply walking along the street. If you are breathing incorrectly, even this simple activity can cause strain. There is a particular way of breathing to a rhythm when walking that makes the experience not only more enjoyable, but much less of a physical effort as well. Walking is incidentally one of the best ways of exercising your body, and I've known many people who have begun to walk as a regular form of exercise once they have tried it with the correct breathing *(see page 38)*.

There are times when you can get so strung up with tension and stress that the result can be a pain or an ache so acute that you simply have to reach for the pain-killing tablets. For occasions such as these, there is a special method of breathing, the Natural Tranquillizing Technique, that you can substitute for those pills (*see page 32*). It is a technique that you have to perform in privacy and quiet, but it is extremely powerful and, in my experience, very successful.

The more you use the simple breathing techniques explained later in this book, the more your confidence will grow as you get used to calming yourself down whenever you need to. As a bonus, you will also find that the quality of your breathing generally improves, without you making a conscious effort. Acquiring the habit of breathing in a relaxed way puts less of a strain on your system and so is healthier.

## THE FEAR OF LETTING GO

In our society, during the process of growing up many of us become increasingly reluctant to show our feelings to those around us. I believe that this has a strong influence on the amount of stress that we will suffer later in our lives. Every time we suppress a spontaneous reaction, every time we hide our emotions, it provides more fuel for our stress time-bomb. Spontaneity, on the other hand, doesn't create any stress or strain. Just think back to the last time that you laughed uncontrollably, or that you had a really good cry. There is usually a great feeling of relief after both of these occasions and that is because you really let yourself go.

Unfortunately, our strong self-protective instincts prevent us from revealing too much of ourselves to others very often. We are afraid that if we do, we may leave ourselves open and vulnerable to attack. We feel much safer if we behave in the reserved way that we think is expected of us, even if it isn't the real us. We have a certain image that we try to project to the outside world, a way of presenting ourselves, and we fear that if we abandon it, even briefly, we may not be able to recover it again. And it is partly also a fear that we are going to make fools of ourselves, to expose the inadequacies that we try so hard to hide from the rest of the world. The interesting thing is that we *all* suffer from these feelings, no matter who we are. I have talked to many highly successful, well-known and respected people and, without exception, they have all admitted to such feelings.

In fact, no alarming consequences will follow if you let go and completely relax. You will still be the same person afterwards that you were before, and you will just carry on with your life. However, there will be differences. You will feel refreshed, revitalized and stronger, and therefore able to actually function more efficiently. If you were pretty stressed you may also, at the end of the relaxation, have slightly altered your perspective on your life. It often happens, after you have completely let go, that the things that seemed incredibly urgent before can now wait a bit. You find that your mind can handle things in a more cool and calculated way and deal with one problem at a time. That problem can then be put behind you when it has been sorted out and you can continue with the next one calmly.

My students often say that a period of deep relaxation seems to them like putting their lives on a hook along with their coats before they begin the session. They let go completely, giving their minds and their bodies a chance for complete rest and relaxation. At the end of the session, they put their coats and their lives back on. Their lives haven't actually changed, and nor have they, but the way that they perceive and handle them has. They feel much more positive and ready to tackle what needs to be tackled but without getting anxious and stressed about it.

Getting used to relaxing completely on a regular basis will enable you to really get in touch with your physical, mental and emotional needs. It will also tune you in to the times in your life when you experience particularly strong stress coupled with exhaustion, and it is then that you need to give yourself a 'total' relaxation break. What I mean by that is the following.

Sometimes after a particular activity, effort or mentally arduous time, we feel quite drained and empty. That is a natural feeling and definite message. It is one that you should go along with if you possibly can, rather than trying to shake yourself out of it which is the common response. At these times, you need to allow yourself to be empty for a while. To be just quiet and still. Not to have to speak, or do anything, or even to think of anything in particular. Allow your mental, physical and emotional energy to flow back gently and fill you up. Learning how to relax completely will help you to do this.

Your ability to let go will increase as you learn, by practising the relaxation techniques, that there is nothing to be afraid of – that all you stand to lose is your stress.

## TAKING CONTROL OF YOUR LIFE

Take two people in exactly the same situation, going through exactly the same experience. One will become stressed and the other will not. This illustrates a basic point made earlier, that stress doesn't just happen to you. You are the one that actually makes it happen. The reaction to stress, therefore, is ultimately your choice, whether or not you are aware of it at the time.

Life is like a roller-coaster, with its ups and downs but, to someone suffering from a lot of stress it can seem a continually uphill struggle. It is all that they can do sometimes simply to get through the day. To such people, it can feel as if stress, strain and problems are their lot in life and that it is due to the kind of person that they are – and that nothing can be done to change that fact. That is absolutely and categorically not the case.

The feeling of being out of control, and not able either to avoid the stress or to react calmly to it, brings with it many other negative feelings, such as weakness, helplessness and inadequacy. This, in turn, causes a sense of shame, and self-recrimination follows. It is therefore important for your sense of self-esteem to know that you can take control of what is happening to you and your life.

It is possible, with a little bit of thought, to avoid some if not all of the situations that you know from past experience make you stressed. Make a list of the worst stresses in your life, and just see, to start off with, whether it isn't possible to eliminate at least one of them. Usually, it doesn't cause the upset or catastrophe that you might have imagined, and the more causes of stress that you are able to avoid, the easier your life becomes.

There is a moment in any potentially stressful situation in which you can decide whether or not you are going to allow the stress and tension to take you over. It is at these moments that you can stop and think of the huge costs involved in terms of your mental and physical health and decide if the situation or problem really warrants you paying that enormous bill. If it doesn't, you can choose, by using certain of the techniques in this book, to take control of things and stay relaxed.

Knowing that you can exercise this control anywhere, anytime, brings with it a growing confidence that will wash over into the whole of your life and, as you will see, the art of taking control is also the art of letting go.

## HOW RELAXATION CAN TRANSFORM YOUR LIFE

If you are suffering from stress, the changes that relaxation can make to your life are really profound. People have described it as being given a new lease of life or of being reborn. When you have suffered from prolonged stress, the removal of it can feel as though a great burden has been lifted from your shoulders.

You can truly transform your life by learning how and when to relax. That means that at least some of the situations and occasions that previously caused you stress can now actually be experienced stress-free, and you can therefore get the most rather than the least out of them.

You will also find that you get on better with people because, the more you relax, the more you become sensitive to those around you and their reactions and responses. It is an unfortunate fact that when you are tense your feelings and thoughts are invariably centred on yourself and it is difficult to communicate well with others. People sense this and can mistakenly assume that you are not concerned about or interested in them. The instant you relax and let go of yourself, a message conveys itself to whoever you are with that your attention is focused on them. Their confidence subsequently grows and that means that they can relax too.

Learning to relax at will can also open up many opportunities for new and wonderful experiences. Often we limit our lives by telling ourselves that we can't do this or that. By using the relaxation techniques, you will gain the ability to 'let go' of such preoccupations and see just how rewarding and satisfying trying out new and adventurous things can be

Life without harmful stress means many things, but in essence it means that you need never again restrict yourself. If a situation is making you feel bad and causing tension and strain, you have the power and the means through re-laxation to change it.

# STRESS CURE A
## Breathing and Relaxation Techniques

The aim of the Stress Cures is to enable you to relax instantly at any time in your life, no matter what you are doing. They will prepare and equip you for almost any situation in which you usually find yourself becoming tense and stressed. You will be able to put specific, learned techniques into action so that your stress will be immediately relieved.

In my experience, the vast majority of stressful situations can be diffused by using the simple Stress Cures given here, provided they are executed correctly.

If you have been suffering with particular stress problems for some time, you may find that although the Stress Cure techniques eliminate the stress, the symptoms later return. When this happens, you simply repeat the techniques again. As you get used to using the Cures, you will automatically be relaxing yourself more and more, and the stress will gradually reduce until it simply ceases to be there.

## WHEN TO USE WHICH TECHNIQUE

The relaxation techniques in this section are all very easy to do and, once you have learned them, you should be able to perform them whenever you are experiencing stress.

There are specific techniques to eliminate stress from different parts of your body, because often tension can cause particular muscle groups to become strained and to tighten up. Many of these techniques are also very valuable in bringing about general stress relief and can be used for this reason alone. These techniques have been listed on *page 30*.

Another recommended way to use this section is as a head-to-toe anti-stress work-out. For details of how to do this and which techniques to use, see *page 30*

Often we are unnecessarily tense in life when we have no need to be, and everyday activities such as sitting, lying, walking and driving are occasions when we could relax much more than we do. You will find specific instructions on how to relax in these situations (*see pages 36–46*).

When we are under tremendous pressure or experiencing particularly bad tension, we can become obsessed and caught up in our spiralling physical reactions to the stress and feel powerless to get out of it. In cases like this, the focus of the mind needs to be diverted onto something external in order to diffuse the situation. The Deviation of Focus Technique (*see page 34*) enables you to do this.

There are also mind-clearing techniques to stop the constant chatter that often goes on inside your head when you want to relax, plus techniques that will show you how to relax your mind and body completely, such as the Total Relaxation with Mind-Clearing Technique (*see page 46*).

Meditation too can be wonderful for concentrating the mind and eliminating disturbing thoughts, but it is a word that sometimes conjures up weird images of people sitting and chanting, or staring at candles for lengthy periods. However, as you will see, that doesn't have to be the case. There are two very easy meditation techniques in this section, a quick one that you can do anytime, anywhere, and a longer and deeper technique that you can practise when you have more time and privacy (*see pages 67–68*). I think you will receive tremendous benefit from both of them.

This first list of techniques can be used both for localized and general relief of stress.
Instant Relaxation for the Face.
Instant Relaxation for the Neck.
Instant Relaxation for the Shoulders.
Instant Relaxation for the Arms, Hands and Fingers.

This next list of techniques can be used as an anti-stress head-to-toe work-out, and practised as often as you like. Follow the order given if you can. Alternatively, you may want to select just two or three which you can then perform as a routine, interchanging the techniques when and if you choose.
**1** The Total Relaxation with Mind-Clearing Technique.
**2** Instant Relaxation for the Arms, Hands and Fingers.
**3** Stomach.
**4** Buttocks.
**5** Legs and Feet.
**6** Deep Meditation Technique.

## 1 OUT-BREATH TECHNIQUE: INSTANT BREATH CONTROL

Breathing has more to do with your ability to relax than anything else. Without doubt, the most important skill that you can learn, if you suffer from stress, is how to take immediate control of your breathing in any situation.

Deep, calm breathing is synonymous with relaxation, whereas stress causes the breathing to quicken up and become more shallow. Unfortunately, the situation can often spiral; the more aware you become of your rapid breathing, the more difficult it seems to be to

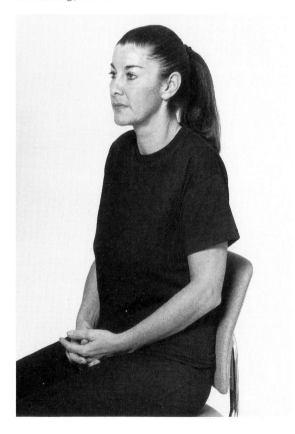

**I** Take a small, gentle breath in through the nose, allowing the diaphragm and waist area to expand a little, but not the chest.

control it and slow it down, so that you simply get more and more stressed. In order to reverse this process and eliminate the stress, we have to find a way to bring the breathing under control and to establish deep, slow breathing.

The following technique is remarkably effective in enabling you to do just that. It can be used in virtually any situation, no matter where you are or what you are doing, and it will bring immediate relief.

When you start the technique, try to resist any inclination to take a really deep in-breath, and concentrate instead on the out-breath. A small in-breath is sufficient, followed by a *really*

*slow* out-breath. You will not be short of breath if you do this because your body will automatically take in enough air without you even being aware of it.

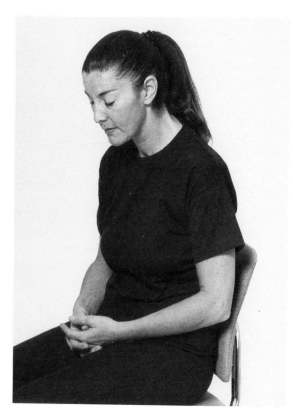

**3** When you are alone or when the situation permits, allow your head to relax gently forwards on the out-breath.

**Note:** *Ideally, this technique should be performed breathing through the nose. However, if for some reason this is difficult for you, it is alright to breathe through the mouth. You will still be receiving substantial benefit from the technique. Try not to have anything tight or restricting around the waist while you are doing it.*

**2** Exhale really slowly through the nose, feeling the diaphragm, stomach and shoulders relaxing. Try to make the out-breath last a minimum of five seconds. Repeat six times if possible.

## 2 THE NATURAL TRANQUILLIZING TECHNIQUE

This technique is very effective and has proved extremely successful when used in stressful situations where people often have to resort to pain-killing tablets. It can also be used to relieve more mild bouts of tension and stress.

In order to release acute tension, three things are required. The first is calm and regular deep breathing, the second is a clear mind, and the third is a relaxed body. This particular technique provides all three.

### How this Technique Works

Your breathing is established in a steady 4-4-4-4 rhythm, counting to yourself at approximately the same speed as seconds. For the first count of four, you are breathing in. For the second count of four, you are holding the breath. For the third count of four, you are breathing out and for the fourth count of four you are remaining without breath, ready to begin again.

Your breathing is being made calm and regular because of the imposed 4-4-4-4 rhythm. Your mind is being cleared of all extraneous thoughts and kept that way because you have to concentrate completely in order not to lose count. Lastly, your body is in a still and relaxed state. The combination of these three elements results in a swift end to your tension and stress and, at the same time, brings about a feeling of calm and tranquillity.

This particular technique requires a little privacy and, as you need to be able to concentrate, try to find a quiet place to do it in.

Loosen the clothing around your waist and neck.
I Sit comfortably, either on a chair or on the floor, with your back straight but not stiff. Place the first two fingers of the right hand on the forehead, the thumb resting lightly on the right nostril and the third and fourth fingers gently closing the left nostril. Then raise the right thumb and take a deep breath through the right nostril for four counts.

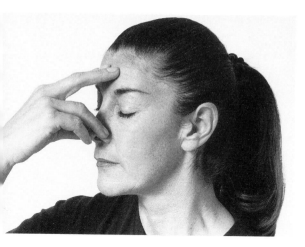

**2** Close both nostrils for four counts.

**3** Release left nostril and exhale slowly for four counts.

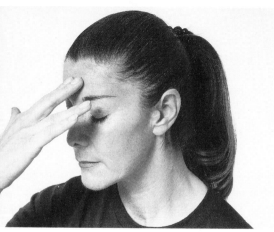

**4** Release both nostrils but stay without breath for four counts. Repeat, but breathing in through the left nostril first. You will then have performed one complete revolution. Repeat a minimum of four revolutions.

As you get used to using this technique, you may want to straighten the top of the back a little and raise your head as you breathe in and, conversely, to let the head and the top of the back relax forward a little as you breathe out. This is a natural inclination and, if it happens, it helps with both the breathing and the relaxing aspect of this technique.

## 3 DEVIATION OF FOCUS TECHNIQUE

When we are very stressed, we can become acutely aware of our own stress reactions but at the same time feel powerless to do anything about them. Our reactions become more marked and we in turn become more obsessed with them. It feels as though the stress is increasing and that there is no way out. It is at times like these that we need to deflect our obsession with ourselves on to something else and we can do this by creating a diversion.

I call this process 'Deviation of Focus' because it entails focusing on something outside rather than inside yourself, and even if this lasts for just a few seconds it is long enough to enable you to let go of the self-obsession that is increasing your stress. You may have to repeat the technique a few moments later and possibly even a third or fourth time, but it really does work.

Imagine that you are talking to somebody and that for some reason you feel very embarrassed. Your embarrassment makes you flush and you try to hide it by not looking at the person. You feel yourself getting hot and sweaty as you struggle to appear calm. In a situation like this, you would immediately focus on, say, the person's nose (do you like the shape?), or on the colour of their hair (is it natural?), or on how many wrinkles they have, and so on. It may seem silly, but when you try it you'll discover that it works. It literally frees you from the grip of the stress.

Let's look at another way that you could use this technique. Imagine that you are in a restaurant and feel stressed because you think that everyone is looking at you. You would use this same Deviation of Focus Technique, but you would focus on something to do with the decor. For example, the curtains (do you like them?) or how many waiters there are.

Another typical example might be at work when you feel inhibited because you think that you are being observed and perhaps assessed. You become clumsy and feel 'all fingers and thumbs'. In this situation you can divert your attention to how many colours a particular person in your office is wearing, or the ages of your colleagues, for example.

Before trying out this technique, it is a good idea to do a little bit of homework. You need to fix in your mind which feature or features you are going to focus on when you next find yourself in this situation, so that you are prepared and you don't panic. You can pick anything that occurs to you, as long as you have thought about it in advance so that you can instantly put the technique into action.

One rule, though, is that if you are face to face with someone, you can't really look directly away from them or he or she will feel rejected. In order for the technique to be undetectable in these sorts of situations, you obviously have to focus on something on or near the person's face. You can use this at any time in your life when the situation calls for it. You will eliminate your stress and nobody will know but you.

### WHAT TO DO

**1** Think about the situations in your life when you experience this type of stress, anxiety, embarrassment.

**2** Write down where each of these situations usually takes place, and then think of three or four features that you could focus on in those situations. Note them down and memorize them.

**3** The next time you find yourself in one of these situations, calmly put the technique into action, concentrating firmly on the fine detail of the object or feature that you are studying.

**4** For even greater effectiveness, combine this with the Out-Breath Technique (see page 30).

This is a typical example of how a stressed person could successfully deviate his or her focus to various parts of another person's head and shoulders without their being aware of it.

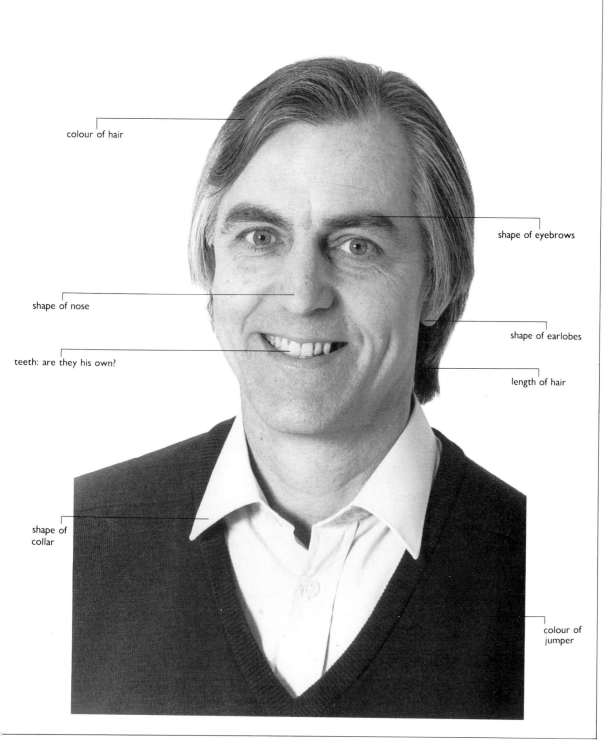

colour of hair

shape of eyebrows

shape of nose

shape of earlobes

teeth: are they his own?

length of hair

shape of
collar

colour of
jumper

## STRESS-FREE AND RELAXED POSITIONS

Everyday activities can impose unnecessary stress and tension. Here is some advice on how to do these things in a more relaxed way.

## 4 SITTING

Although sitting would appear to be a semi-relaxed position in itself, we do not always take advantage of this by relaxing as fully as we might. It is often the case that much of the time we spend sitting, far from being in a relaxed state, our bodies can be causing unnecessary strain and stress. We may be sitting to do a job of work or in an easy chair, supposedly relaxing, and we can unknowingly put our bodies into awkward positions, using muscles that we don't really need. This sets up tension and leads to tiredness. We may not realize that we are doing this to ourselves, but just observe other people when they are sitting; see how they position their bodies and twist and strain and fidget. Most of us do the same thing.

Whether you are at work or in a social setting, it is possible to re-adjust your sitting position to your physical advantage. This applies even if you have to work sitting in a fixed position for most of the day, especially if your head and eyeline don't move a great deal. This type of static positioning of the body for long periods, as with people who work at VDU screens, typewriters, architects' planning boards and so on, can cause considerable physical stress and strain. The same applies with any other relatively still seated occupation.

### FORMAL CHAIR

**1** The two examples above show the incorrect way to sit. The muscles are tensed needlessly and the breathing apparatus is being impaired, causing stress.

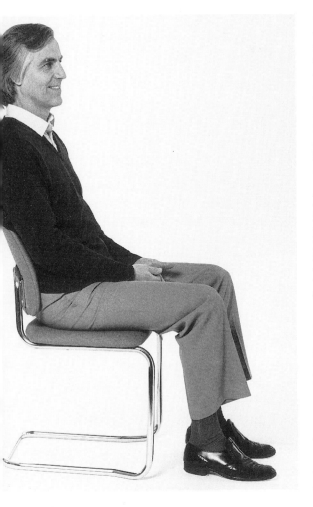

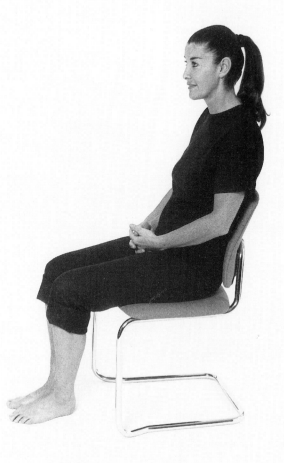

**2** This is the correct way to sit whenever possible to give you comfort and maximum relaxation.

If the seat of your chair is level, it is a constant strain for your back to have to lean forward slightly all the time, which is the most common work position. If you suffer from pain in the neck, shoulders or back after sitting for prolonged periods, then try tilting the seat of your chair or stool forward by putting something under the back legs such as thick telephone books. This will tilt the base of your back forward giving you better support and relieving the strain.

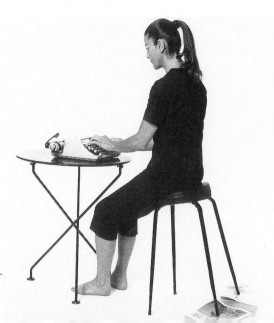

## ARMCHAIR

1 Incorrect way to sit (slumped).

2 Correct way to sit and relax.

## WHAT TO DO

**1** Whether you are in an easy chair or a more formal chair, you need to sit as squarely as possible. That means with the legs open, not crossed, and the feet planted firmly on the floor.

**2** Your back should be as straight as possible, so don't slump, and wriggle your bottom as far into the back of the chair as you can.

**3** Try to consciously relax your shoulders and arms.

**4** In order to relax, you must be able to breathe freely and deeply. That means allowing your diaphragm to expand and contract as you breathe in and out. Try, therefore, to wear clothing that is loose around the waist or, alternatively, something that you can loosen easily.

Check your position with the illustrations showing the wrong and the right way to sit.

## 5 WALKING

Most of us spend at least some time in our lives walking to get from A to B, but we rarely give it much thought. I think that we should seriously consider how we walk because it can either be a wonderfully relaxing exercise for the body and the mind, or it can produce muscle strain, stress and tension.

Walking correctly as a way of exercising and keeping fit can be beneficial in all sorts of ways. It works the muscles and joints of the legs, feet and toes. It improves circulation. It works the heart and lungs. It improves balance, co-ordination and stamina. It is safe, unlike many of the more violent forms of exercise. It is cheap. Anyone can do it no matter where they are and, on top of all that, you have access to fresh air as well.

All these benefits can be yours, but it does

I The incorrect body position when walking.

2 The correct, relaxed way to walk.

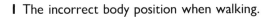

mean becoming more conscious of the way that you walk and then correcting it if necessary. This applies if you are simply going shopping or to the bus stop because even on short walks you can still make a significant difference to your general health and stress level.

It is important to hold your body in the correct position while walking, and to breathe in the right way. Wrong positioning of the body and faulty breathing can cause strain, tiredness and exhaustion. So follow these instructions whenever you have to walk anywhere and get the most, rather than the least, out of it.

### WHAT TO DO

I Walk with the back straight but not stiff, your head erect and your neck, shoulders, arms and hands relaxed.

2 If you are carrying things, try whenever possible to distribute the weight evenly.

3 Feel as though your diaphragm and rib cage are leading the way but without actually pushing them out in an exaggerated manner. This simply keeps the back in the right position and allows freedom for the correct breathing.

4 Walk briskly, establishing a definite rhythm.

5 You are now ready to incorporate the correct breathing. On every second step, blow the breath out sharply through your mouth, as though you are going to whistle. Don't think of taking the in-breath at all, it will just happen automatically.

# 6 DRIVING

Driving must be one of the most stressful occupations in life and the stress is there no matter how short or long the journey is.

A certain amount of physical and mental stress is unavoidable and indeed necessary when driving, but we also create a lot of added stress. There are techniques that can both reduce and eliminate this unnecessary stress.

Let's look first of all at the physical stress of driving. The body is kept in a set position, with certain of your muscles being held tense and taut. Working from head to toe, your neck, shoulder, back, arm and hand muscles are all being constantly used simply to keep the top of your body in this fixed position. Moving further down the body, your thigh, calf and feet muscles are working to a slightly lesser degree, but you can't relax them because they always have to be ready for immediate action. The physical strain then is quite substantial. Add to this other common physical factors such as the periodic tensing of the stomach muscles when something unexpected happens, eyestrain, especially on long journeys and at night, and of course tiredness and fatigue.

Mentally, too, you are under intense and unremitting stress while you are driving because your concentration needs to be one hundred per cent all the time. As well as this, you have all the other common stressful factors to contend with, such as worry and anxiety about arriving late, bad traffic conditions, inconsiderate or stupid drivers, and the million and one other frustrating things that can affect you. So there is no doubt that driving is stressful. However, the following tips should help to make driving a more relaxed and safer experience.

The wrong way to sit when driving. Shoulders hunched over the wheel and limbs obviously over tensed.

## WHAT TO DO

1 Your physical position plays a large part in how stressed you get, so check your usual driving position with those shown in the pictures and correct yours if necessary.

2 Turn it to your advantage every time you are forced to stop at, say, traffic lights. This gives you the perfect opportunity to use relaxation techniques for specific parts of the body, depending where you feel stiff and tense.

For example, when you are stuck at the lights, and your shoulders feel a little stiff, do the Instant Relaxation for the Shoulders Technique (see page 56). It only takes a few seconds, and you will feel immediate relief. A subsequent stop could give you the chance to do the Instant Relaxation for the Neck Technique (see page 52) to eliminate the stiffness in your neck. At a later stop you could relieve the tension in the arms and fingers (see page 58).

The correct driving position. Remember to always wear a safety belt. Shoulders relaxed, using back of seat for good support of the spine.

**3** Get used to doing a quick Body Check (*see page 66*) every now and again whilst driving. This means becoming aware if you are gripping any muscles unnecessarily tightly and letting them go a bit if you are.

**4** If you are getting really angry and frustrated at road conditions or other drivers, try the Out-Breath Technique (*see page 30*). It will instantly calm you down. Use any other of the appropriate techniques from this section in the same way.

**5** Since most people get stressed when driving because they are late, a good habit to get into is always to leave a few minutes early.

**6** If possible, try not to eat a big meal before driving, especially if you are going on a long journey, as this can make you feel drowsy, and that of course can be very dangerous. Likewise, drinking alcohol before driving should be avoided for the same reason. If you do feel tired or drowsy you should immediately pull over, park and either get out of the car to stretch and walk around a bit to clear your head, or have a short nap. This of course doesn't apply to motorway driving where it would be dangerous to stop except at a service area. It will also help to keep you awake if you make sure that you always have fresh air coming into the car.

**7** Try to loosen your clothing a little bit around the waist so that your breathing will be unrestricted and relaxed.

## 7 LYING DOWN

**1** How not to lie if you want to relax.

**2** A better and more beneficial relaxing position.

However stressed we may be in the daytime, we console ourselves with the comforting thought that, whatever else happens when we actually lie down, either to sleep or simply to rest, we will be able to relax completely. However, this is certainly not always the case for many people.

First let's look at what might be preventing you from getting the benefits that you should be getting when you relax during the day.

Your body position is all important, and this is obviously going to be influenced by where and how you are lying. If, for example, you are on a squashy sofa, it may look very comfortable but, if it doesn't support your weight sufficiently, some of your muscles will be straining to maintain your position. The same applies to lying in an armchair with your feet propped up on a footstool. If the stool is too far away, or if the level is lower than that of the chair, you will have to strain to keep the legs there, so you need to think about this if you can before you settle down to relax. The arm of a sofa always looks like the ideal headrest, but it can often push your head too far forward towards your chest. This not only causes back and neck strain but also constricts the throat and chest area, making breathing difficult.

The pictures show both the wrong and right way to relax.

## WHAT TO DO

**1** Wherever you are resting, try to lie with the back and head well supported on a firm surface. The flatter the surface, the better.

**2** Loosen your clothing, especially around your waist and neck.

**3** Relax your arms and hands and place them in a position where you won't be inclined to fidget.

**4** Now close your eyes.

**5** Concentrate on the Out-Breath (*see page 30*) and with each out-breath feel the body sinking further and further down.

**6** If you wish, you can now incorporate the Total Relaxation with Mind-Clearing Technique *(see page 46)*.

**7** Try to stay resting like this for a minimum of fifteen minutes.

*Note: The best position of all as far as total relaxation is concerned, whether used day or night, is the one shown overleaf. It should be done either lying on the floor or on the bed. If you are stressed, I would encourage you to try it because it is an extremely effective position for the relief of stress.*

---

# 8 SLEEPING

We all need a good night's sleep and if we don't get it we become irritable, find it difficult to concentrate, get depressed and so on. On the physical side, if we are tired, we get aches and pains and are more vulnerable to diseases and infections.

People have very differing requirements when it comes to how much sleep they need, and you are the only one that can really gauge this. Some people feel fine on just five or six

hours a night, and others need eight or nine or more. More important than the number of hours that you sleep, however, is the actual quality of your sleep.

If you consistently wake up feeling drained or worn out, then the chances are that the quality of your sleep is poor and you are consequently not getting the physical and mental relaxation that you need. There are three main reasons for this – your body, your mind and maybe even your bed.

## Your Body Position

The position of your body when sleeping, can either help or hinder you from getting a good night's sleep, and we don't necessarily choose the most beneficial position. People adopt all manner of positions, many of which started way back in childhood and have become habitual. One of the most common is the foetal position. This is where you are curled up on your side as you were in the womb. The problem with this position is that you are crushing the arm, shoulder and leg that your weight is on, preventing good circulation. Your breathing apparatus is also being constricted since your shoulders are hunched together, and your neck and head are bent at strange angles because of the pillow. Keeping the head in this strained position all night can cause a stiff neck and can also push your spine out of alignment causing back problems. This is especially true if your back is weak.

Lying on the stomach, although another very common sleeping position, has its problems as well. Once again, the breathing apparatus is constricted and, if you are using pillows, the head and neck are bent at an even worse angle than when the body is lying on its side. There are, of course, many other common sleeping positions but, in my opinion, they all, to a greater or lesser extent, fail to allow the body to relax completely.

The ideal position is the one shown in the picture because every muscle in your body can relax. Your lungs and diaphragm are totally free from any pressure or constraint and can function efficiently. Your blood circulation is unimpaired, and your spine and head are well supported.

---

## TOTAL RELAXATION BODY POSITION

If, as for a lot of people, this is not a 'natural' sleeping position for you, try to resist the temptation to dismiss it because, if you are a stress sufferer, the benefits of relaxing your body this way are enormous. It is possible to get yourself used to the position gradually, especially if you use the Total Relaxation with Mind-Clearing Technique which follows. You will find that you are able to spend longer and longer periods resting like this. Eventually, you may find it so comfortable that you will not want to change it and will be falling asleep in it.

## How About the Mind?

Often it is your mind that is your worst enemy when you are trying to get to sleep. It can seem that, whatever you do, you simply can't switch it off. If you have been through this you will know that it can be a most distressing experience. There you are in your bed, dog tired, desperately wanting to get to sleep, but your mind refuses to stop. Your frustration and stress mount as you realise that the night is

**This is the best possible position for sleeping.**

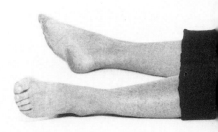

swiftly passing and you have progressively less and less time to sleep. You dread to think how you are going to feel in the morning.

Don't despair! By practising the following Mind-Clearing Technique you will be able to clear your mind at will. Use it in bed when you are ready to sleep, in combination with the Total Relaxation body position illustrated, and you can learn how first to direct and concentrate the mind and subsequently to let your mind and body go.

## A Word about Your Bed

If you really want to get the best quality rest that you can when sleeping, then your body has to be properly supported. For this you need to have a firm mattress and to use just one flattish pillow. What you are trying to avoid is having your back curving downwards into the bed, and if you have a soft bed plus more than one pillow, that is exactly what will happen. If this applies to you, and you don't want the expense of buying a new bed, try putting a stiff board underneath your mattress. It costs very little and can do wonders for your health and sleeping comfort. Here are several additional tips that will help you to a good night's sleep.

## WHAT TO DO

**1** Don't eat late. Try to have your evening meal a minimum of two-and-a-half to three hours before you go to bed.

**2** Don't rush around the house doing things for an hour or so before retiring as this will only wake you up. Try, if you have jobs that must be done, to do them slowly and lazily.

**3** If you read, listen to music or watch the television late at night, try not to choose anything too stimulating or intellectually demanding.

**4** Practice the Total Relaxation with Mind-Clearing Technique on the following pages.

If you haven't slept well for quite some time, you may find that you have to get used to practising the techniques a bit before they can work completely for you. If you do not immediately go off to sleep, or find yourself waking in the middle of the night, the worst thing that you can do is to lie in bed, agonizing over the fact that you can't sleep. This will only increase your tension and stress. Instead, try the following. Give yourself, say, fifteen to twenty minutes to do something constructive. This may entail jotting down notes about what you have to do the next day or at some time in the future, or even getting out of bed and making yourself a warm drink. It often happens that after taking this short break you can return to bed and repeat the technique and go off to sleep peacefully.

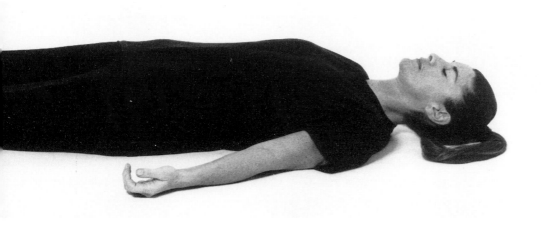

# 9 TOTAL RELAXATION WITH MIND-CLEARING TECHNIQUE

This is without doubt the most perfect relaxation position that I have ever found. Use it whenever you want to achieve total relaxation either during the day or in bed at night.

The body is completely unconstrained and therefore virtually every single muscle is at rest. Your respiratory system can function at optimum level, as can your blood circulation; your back and head are perfectly supported.

Although there is nothing complicated about this position, it is very important that you take notice of details such as the positioning of the hands, feet and head, even though these might seem trivial. They are really relevant to the degree of relaxation that you will receive, for the following reasons.

If the hands are positioned with the palms and fingertips turned downwards, there is a tendency to want to touch the floor or the bed and fidget, which affects the relaxation of the shoulders, arms, hands and fingers. Whereas with the palms turned upwards, that doesn't happen. A second reason for the positioning of the hands in this way is because it gives you a sensation of more openness and freedom around the chest and diaphragm areas.

**Note:** *Obviously you cannot read the instructions and perform this technique at the same time. Read through the instructions until you think you have more or less memorized them before you start.*

*You may find to start off with, as you go through this technique, that your mind is wandering away from the part of the body that you are meant to be concentrating on. Don't worry about this. Let your mind wander anywhere it likes for a few moments and then just gently bring it back to where you were. This will occur less and less as time goes on.*

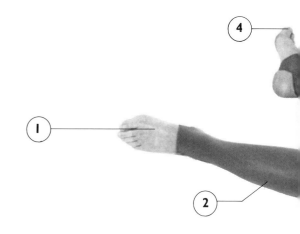

| | | | |
|---|---|---|---|
| 1 | left foot | 10 | left forearm |
| 2 | left calf | 11 | left upper arm |
| 3 | left thigh | 12 | right hand |
| 4 | right foot | 13 | right forearm |
| 5 | right calf | 14 | right upper arm |
| 6 | right thigh | 15 | forehead |
| 7 | diaphragm | 16 | eyes |
| 8 | chest area | 17 | mouth |
| 9 | left hand | | |

## WHAT TO DO

1 Study the picture carefully and note the position of the head, hands, legs and feet. Then try to learn and memorize the numbered parts of the body.
2 Wear very comfortable and loose clothing, especially around the waist and throat.
3 If you are doing this in the daytime, try to find somewhere quiet where you won't be disturbed.
4 Don't rush when you are ready to perform this technique, just lie down and get comfortable.
5 Place the hands, feet and head as shown.
6 Close your eyes and simply rest for a few moments.
7 Try to visualize how your body looks lying in this position. (Imagine you are looking at a photograph of yourself).

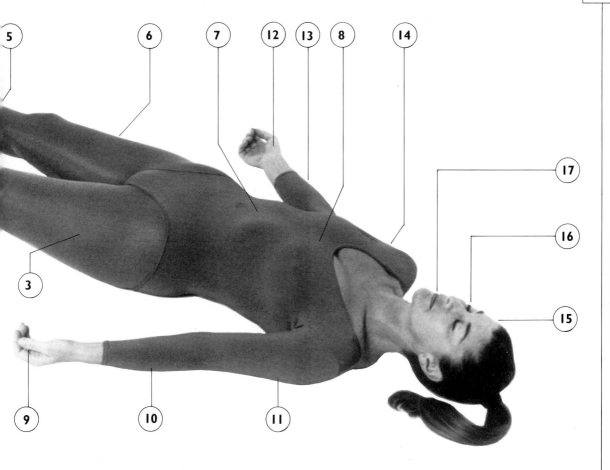

**8** Don't move a muscle but, with your eyes still closed, begin with your left foot. Concentrate purely on how it looks in the position that it is in. Notice how the toes and toe joints look, and any other feature that comes into your mind. Stay with these images for approximately thirty seconds and then let go of them.

**9** Move up to the left calf, and repeat the procedure. Imagine how the flesh at the back of the calf is being squashed down because of the weight of your leg, and the shape it is therefore making. Notice anything else about your left calf that comes into your mind. Hold those images there for approximately thirty seconds, then let them go and continue with the left thigh, and so on as indicated by the numbers in the photograph.

**10** Gradually work right through the body until you reach the mouth.

**11** Concentrate on the diaphragm area once more, and your out-breath. Every time you exhale, picture and feel your diaphragm sinking down slowly. Don't force this to happen, just be aware of it. Concentrate purely on the slowness of the out-breath and the in-breath will happen automatically. You only need to take in very little breath.

**12** Count a minimum of twenty slow out-breaths. Then you have reached the end of this technique, which should take at least fifteen minutes.

**13** When using this technique to get to sleep at night, you may well find that you fall asleep before you complete the technique. That, of course, doesn't matter.

## INSTANT RELAXATION FOR SPECIFIC PARTS OF THE BODY

### 10 EYES

We are constantly having to subject our eyes to stress and strain and, unfortunately, since most of us can't change our lives and working environments significantly, a certain amount of eyestrain is unavoidable. This technique relieves and relaxes the eyes and should be used as often as possible. Eyestrain can be caused by many factors such as the following, all of which may lead to sore eyes, headaches, irritability, and fatigue.

Working at a VDU console.
Studying or reading for long periods of time, or when you are tired.
Watching television.
Living with or working in very bright or fluorescent lighting.
Living with or working in dim lighting.

### Tips for Avoiding Eyestrain

• If you work at a VDU or watch a lot of television, look away from the screen periodically or close your eyes for a few moments.
• If you are reading or studying, try to have a good source of light coming from behind you and directed over your shoulder at your work.
• Don't do close work in dim lighting.
• Don't read in bed with the wrong lighting.
• Try not to rub your eyes even if they are irritating you.
• An eye bath helps to clear the eyes of dust.
• If you have the time and your eyes are really sore, this strange and unconventional tip really works wonders. Place two used, cold teabags over your eyes, lie flat and relax for about fifteen minutes.

**1** Sit with your head erect and widen the eyes as much as you can.

**4** Roll your eyes down, keeping your head still, focus and hold for five.

**2** Keeping the head still, raise your eyes to look at the ceiling. Hold it for a count of five.

**3** Roll your eyes slowly around to your right, focus and hold it for a count of five.

**5** Roll your eyes to your left, focus, hold for five. Roll upwards again and repeat in other direction.

**6** Close your eyes, let your head and shoulders relax and rest for a few moments.

## 11 FACE

We don't usually think of the face as a part of the body that needs either exercise or relaxation, but why not? There are, after all, muscles there as in the rest of the body and, to keep them healthy, they need to be used regularly.

As children, we worked our facial muscles much more than we do as adults. This is partly because our facial expressions decrease as we grow up and we learn, unfortunately, to show less emotion. We do often 'wear' a special expression in public and try to 'look pleasant', but holding the face fixed in this way can cause a great deal of muscle strain. Having limited movement, it becomes very set, consequently looking and feeling tense. So it is very relaxing physically and mentally to let both the muscles and the expression go.

There are several ways of doing this, but this particular technique exercises the face, improving the muscle tone and the circulation. It has the added benefit of releasing a lot of pent-up tension when used with the appropriate breathing.

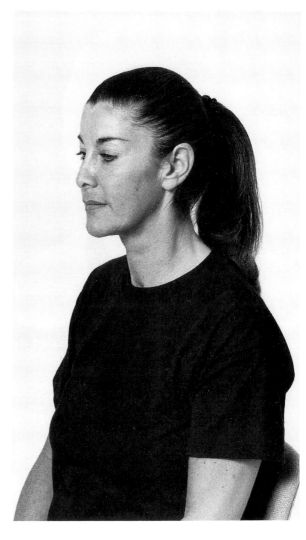

**I** Sit comfortably with the back and head straight, and arms and hands relaxed in your lap.

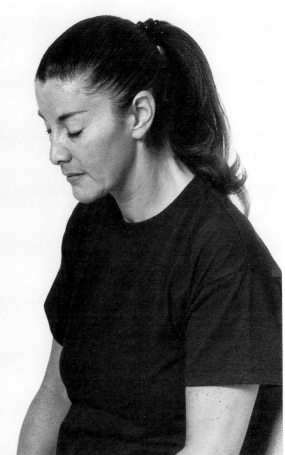

**2** Breathe in deeply through the nose first, then widen the eyes, open the mouth as much as you can and breathe out with a long HAAAA! sound. Try to make the out-breath last for five seconds or more.

**3** Relax with the eyes closed and the face completely expressionless for a few moments, breathing normally.

Repeat five more times.

## 12 NECK

There are specific parts of the body where stress seems to manifest itself more commonly than other areas, and the neck is just such an example. The pain can be excruciating, and it can feel as though there is nothing that you can do to relieve it.

### WHAT TO DO

This technique is not only good at instantly removing the pain and stiffness, but you can do it whenever you need to during the day as it only takes three or four minutes of your time.

Move your head really slowly and gently when rolling it round and don't be tempted to push it over further than its own weight is taking it. The object is not to make the head go over a long way because, without you doing any pushing, its own weight is sufficient to 'open the neck joints' and work out the stress and tension.

**1** Sit and relax the head, shoulders, arms and hands, and close your eyes.

**2** Slowly roll your head round to your left side. Stop and simply let the head rest there for a slow count of five.

**3** Slowly roll your head round to the back and let it rest for a count of five. Your mouth can be open or closed, whichever feels most comfortable.

**4** Slowly roll your head round to your right and let it rest for a count of five.

**5** Turn your head as though you were looking in profile to the right of you.

**6** Lower your chin towards your shoulder.

**7** Push your chin gently downwards as you bring your head back to the starting position.

Repeat the movement in the other direction and, if you have time, do it once again on both sides, then stay with the head relaxed and the eyes closed for a few moments before continuing with your life.

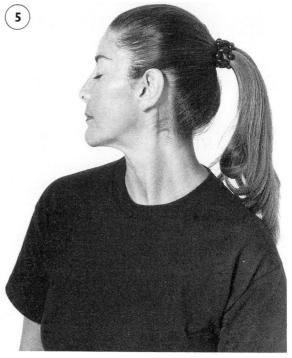

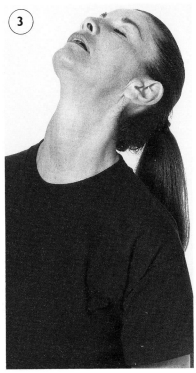

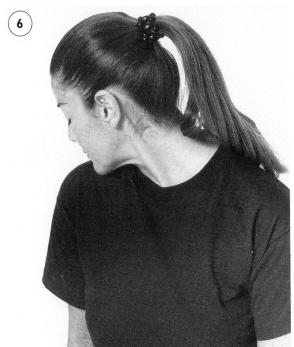

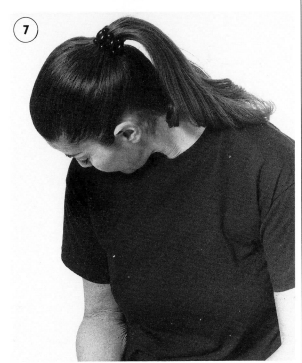

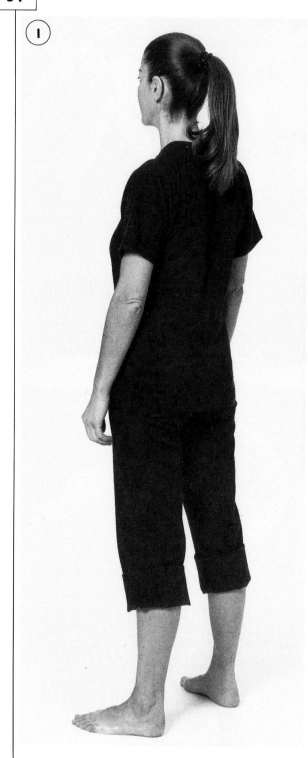

① ② ③

## 13 TOP OF THE BACK

This technique has proved extremely effective in removing the tension from the top of the back and between the shoulder blades. Anyone who has suffered from this particular type of stress pain will know that it can be quite agonizing. It also seems very difficult to do anything about because you can't get to it to massage it. This procedure does that for you, but you must follow the instructions carefully and precisely.

Try to do it in privacy, if possible, bearing in mind that it will only take a few minutes.

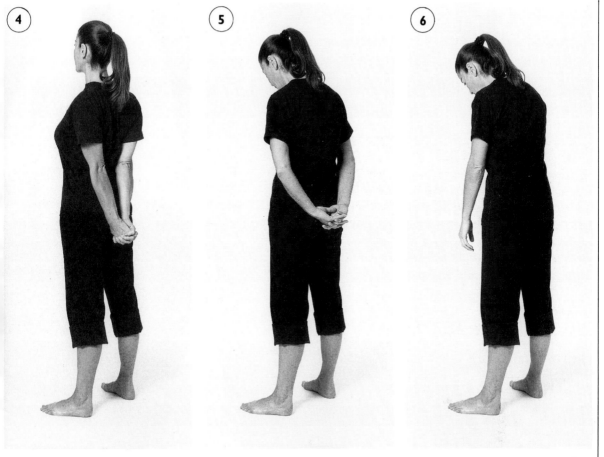

## WHAT TO DO

**1** Stand with your feet square, your back and head straight and your arms hanging loosely at your sides.

**2** Interlock your fingers behind you and then close the palms tightly together, if you can.

**3** Take a deep breath in through the nose as you make a big rotating movement with your shoulders, taking them forwards, up to your ears, over, back and down.

**4** Straighten your elbows as much as you can comfortably. Hold the position and the breath for a slow count of five.

**5** Exhale slowly and let your elbows bend, the palms of the hands open a bit and your head and shoulders relax forward. Rest for a few moments breathing normally and then repeat the technique a further five times.

**6** Let the arms and hands gently fall open and relax like this for a minute or so at the end, then straighten up slowly and return to your normal activities.

***Note:*** *If it is uncomfortable to close the palms of your hands tightly together, it is fine to execute the technique with the palms open. As you practise more and more, the palms will come closer together.*

## 14 SHOULDERS

Stiff and aching shoulders are one of the more
common results of stress. The reason why this
is so is that when we get tense we tend to hold
our shoulders hunched up or stiff without
realizing it. We sometimes maintain this
'abnormal' position for very long periods, and
the result is often acute pain in the muscles and
joints.

   This shoulder relaxing movement will release
the physical tension and, if executed with the
correct breathing, will also bring about a general
relaxation and 'letting go'. However, in order to
get this double benefit it is important that you
take the deep breath at the right point, hold it
as instructed, and then let it out really slowly.

   A big plus with this technique is that it can
be used as often as you like during the day,
whenever you feel stiffness or aching in the
general area of the shoulders. It only takes a few
minutes and it brings tremendous and rapid
relief.

**I** Sit with the back straight but not stiff, and your
arms and hands relaxed.

**2** Take a deep breath in through the nose and, at the same time, rotate your shoulders forward and up to your ears.

Hold the position and the breath for a count of five.

**3** Exhale really slowly, gently relaxing the head and shoulders forward. Wait a few moments and repeat. Perform six times in all, relaxing afterwards as shown for a minute or so.

## 15 ARMS, HANDS AND FINGERS

We can sometimes create and hold a lot of tension in this area of our bodies. Many of us unknowingly grip our arm, hand and finger muscles when we don't need to. Our fingers are seldom at rest, and even when the body is relaxing, we continue to fiddle and fidget. This tension may not make its presence known with pain and stiffness, as happens with other areas of the body, but it can nevertheless greatly contribute to your stress level.

There are many habits born of stress and tension, and making unnecessary gestures with the arms and hands is one of the most common. If you know that you do this and it worries you, I would encourage you to try this technique because it not only relaxes the arms, hands and

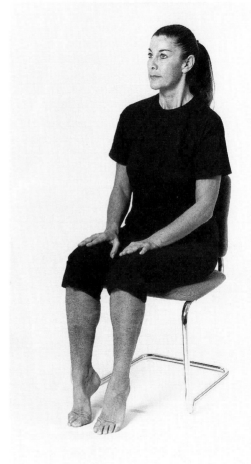

**1** Sit with the back and head straight but not stiff, and the hands and arms resting palms downward as shown in the picture.

**2** Take a deep breath in through the nose and raise the heels.

fingers, but it also gives you an awareness of how they feel when they are totally relaxed. It then becomes easier for you to recognize when they are tense, and to let them go at will when you find yourself fiddling and want to stop.

*Note: This technique is also immensely valuable when used purely for general stress removal, as the specific breathing procedure, coupled with the movement, results in overall relief and relaxation.*

**3** Blow the breath out strongly through the mouth and, at the same time, extend your arms and spread your fingers really wide, pushing down hard on your knees. Hold the position and the breath for a count of five.

**4** Take a second deep breath in through the nose and, as you blow the breath out more slowly this time, relax the hands, arms, shoulders, legs and feet. Close your eyes and wait for a few moments, breathing normally. Repeat a further five times.

# 16 STOMACH

We saw earlier that the wish to conceal self-consciousness often makes us grip parts of the body that aren't visible to others and of these the stomach is the most common. We feel a sense of security in the knowledge that as these areas can't be seen, nor can our tension and anxiety. That doesn't usually work, however, because when we are tense and stressed we are unconsciously giving out many other signs and signals as well.

When we tense and hold the stomach muscles it dramatically increases our original stress because it affects and greatly restricts our ability to breathe normally. The diaphragm is automatically squeezed when we tense up, and this prevents the gentle expansion and contraction of that area that is needed for normal breathing. Consequently, our breathing becomes more difficult and laboured and this in turn leads us to worry that we are not taking in enough breath. We begin to take quicker and sharper breaths, knowing that our anxiety is becoming more obvious, and this leads us to grip the stomach muscles even more in an attempt to calm down. Of course the reverse happens, and the breathing becomes even more limited. We start to panic, get hot and sweaty and try even harder to disguise the fact. Our stress level goes up and up.

We need, therefore, to be able to take control in this type of situation and release the gripped stomach muscles at will; this in turn will bring about normal breathing, relaxation and the subsequent elimination of stress. Having this ability will also mean that next time, at the slightest suggestion of stress, we will be able to prevent the muscles tensing and simply not allow it to happen.

Tensing and gripping the stomach can have other harmful consequences besides the very unpleasant panicky sensation that I have just described. It can also interfere seriously with the digestive system. The body is involved in processing and digesting food not only when we are actually eating but also long afterwards. If we disturb these processes by periodically gripping the stomach muscles, all sorts of unpleasant and painful conditions can result.

Unfortunately, a common habit among stressed people is to tense the stomach when they eat and to bolt their food. However, both of these habits can be broken and eating can return to being the relaxed pleasure that it should be.

The following technique will teach you how to release the stomach muscles at will, thereby allowing you to relax, breathe normally and eliminate your stress and tension.

## WHAT TO DO

**1** If you feel the stomach muscles tightening when you are stressed, exhale slowly, letting go of the muscles and, at the same time, allowing the waist area to expand. Repeat as many times as you need.
**2** Practise the procedure illustrated (*see instructions below*) when you have some time and privacy, loosening your clothing around the waist before you start. It will increase your awareness and control over these muscles and relax you at the same time.

*Right:*
**1** Stand with the back and head straight but not stiff, and the hands and arms relaxed.
**2** Take a deep breath and pull the stomach muscles right in and up underneath the rib cage.
Hold the position and the breath for a count of five.

Exhale slowly relaxing the stomach, head, neck and shoulders. Rest like this for a few moments, breathing normally, and then repeat a further five times.

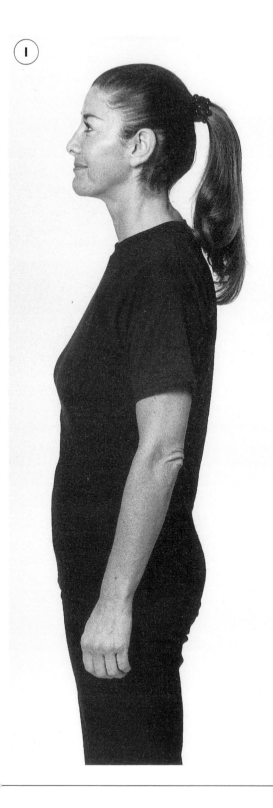

## 17 BUTTOCKS

When trying to conceal tension, annoyance or
stress we often grip the buttock muscles tightly.
This usually also entails gripping the leg muscles
as well. Of course we do this without being
aware of it, but the more we tighten up anywhere
in our bodies, the greater our stress and muscle
fatigue will be. If we can therefore become
conscious of when we do this and subsequently
release those muscles, the tension and overall
stress will be instantly reduced.

### *WHAT TO DO*

**1** If you feel your buttocks tightening when you are
stressed, make a conscious effort to squeeze the
muscles even more. Hold them tense for a few
moments and really let them go.

**2** Practise the following technique when you have
some time to yourself and it will enable you to
become more aware of just when you are tensing
those muscles and how it feels to let them go
completely.

**1** Lie on the floor, relaxed. Take a deep breath and grip the buttocks in and up.
Hold the position and the breath for a count of five.

**2** Exhale as you lower and relax all the muscles. Rest for a few moments, breathing normally, and then repeat a further five times.

## STAGE 1

**1** Sit on a chair with your back straight but not stiff, and hands relaxed in your lap.

**2** Extend your right leg, locking the knee and pointing the toes. Hold the position still for a count of five.

## 18 LEGS AND FEET

In the course of a day, considerable pressure can build up in the legs and feet, since we are upright for most of the time, either standing or carrying around our body weight. This in itself can lead to the very common sensation of aching legs and feet.

Another reason for aches and pains in the legs and feet is the fact that we can grip the muscles in our thighs, calves and toes involuntarily when we are feeling nervous or stressed. Often, just taking the weight off our feet doesn't totally relieve the ache in the muscles and joints, but working specific muscles and then gently letting them go, as with these techniques, does seem to be more effective in

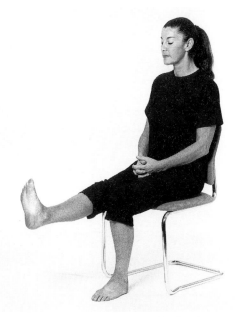

**3** Flex the foot back, pushing the heel away from you, but continue to keep the knee straight. Hold the position still for a count of five and then gently return the right leg to the starting position and let it relax. Repeat the technique with the left leg and then repeat three more times with each leg.

releasing the tension and strain in the legs and feet, as well as improving the circulation.

Choice of footwear has a great influence on how much strain we put on our legs and feet. High-heeled shoes, for example, throw the full body weight onto the toes and constrict them, preventing good circulation and requiring you to tense specific muscles in the calves and thighs. High heels, incidentally, can also damage and strain the back, because it is being permanently pushed forward into an unnatural position. Tight shoes are also bad as they constrict the feet and toes, affecting both the joints and the circulation. Therefore, the more comfortable your footwear is, the less damage and stress you will cause yourself.

Begin with Stage 1 of the technique, shown in the pictures, and when you have done it a few times and can memorize it, you may like to incorporate Stage 2.

## STAGE 2

**1** Extend your right leg as in Stage 1, with the knee straight and toes pointed. Then interlock your fingers underneath your leg to keep it steady.

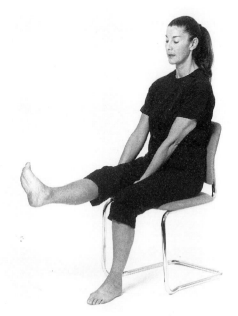

**2** Slowly rotate your foot in the clockwise direction six times. Relax your leg and repeat with the left leg.

**3** Take care to go to the extreme points of the circle.

## 19 THE BODY CHECK

Once learned, the following technique can be done quickly, anytime, anywhere, and will enable you to instantly release your body tension and, therefore, to relax and substantially reduce or even totally eliminate your stress.

Essentially what you are doing is systematically working from your head down to your feet, letting go of any tense muscles. In order to do this, you need to be able to distinguish whether your muscles are tense or relaxed. Some people can do this automatically whilst others find it a little more difficult. If the latter applies to you, you will find it a great help if you practise the following techniques for Instant Relaxation for Specific Parts of the Body:

Face (*see page 50*).
Neck (*see page 52*).
Shoulders (*see page 56*).
Arms, Hands and Fingers (*see page 58*).
Stomach (*see page 60*).
Buttocks (*see page 62*).
Legs and Feet (*see page 64*).

### *WHAT TO DO*

Practise the Body Check in advance a few times, so that it becomes very familiar to you. It will take you only seconds to perform. Then, no matter what situation you are in, whenever you feel the slightest sign of tension or stress, immediately implement the technique, working right through the body from head to toe, as instructed.

**1** Concentrate on your face for a few seconds and see if it feels as though the muscles are being held tense. Pay particular attention to your mouth and your forehead. Let the muscles go, and be aware of the face feeling more relaxed.

**2** Move down to your neck and check how you are holding it. If it is unnecessarily bent over or twisted, straighten it up.

**3** Check your shoulders and see if you can let them drop and relax. The relief you will feel with this can be quite dramatic.

**4** Think about what your arms, hands and fingers are doing and then try to release any unnecessarily gripped muscles. This may possibly mean altering your position slightly.

**5** Next, check your stomach muscles. If you are gripping them, let them go.

**6** Do the same with the buttock muscles.

**7** Check your legs and feet, paying particular attention to whether you are unnecessarily gripping the muscles in your thighs. Also, whether your knees are tightly locked when they have no need to be, and whether your toes are curled. Let go and relax your legs and feet, changing your position if necessary.

## MIND-CLEARING AND RELAXATION TECHNIQUES

Sometimes, if you are tense, it can seem impossible to concentrate. You keep thinking of other things and problems and no matter how many times you try to get rid of those thoughts they keep coming back.

## 20 QUICK MEDITATION – ANYTIME, ANYWHERE

If you wish to cut out extraneous thoughts, and rein in your mind and quieten it down in order to devote your energy to the job in hand, try this quick, simple and effective meditation technique. It only takes five minutes and can be done anywhere.

### WHAT TO DO

**1** Sit comfortably and look at any fixed, still object that you like, making sure that the object is directly in front of you.

Stay absolutely still, taking in virtually all the details of the object for five minutes. Then briefly close your eyes and return to your day.

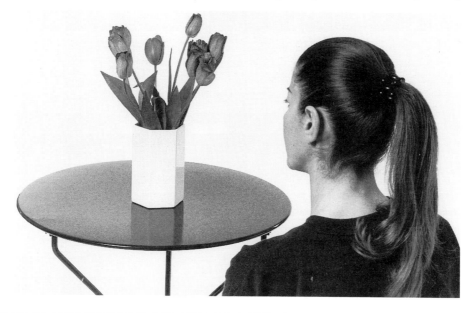

**I** Perform the Out-Breath Technique (*see page 30*).　**2** Perform the Shoulders Technique (*see page 56*).

## 21 DEEP MEDITATION

Although this is called deep meditation, don't be alarmed – you will not have to chant or burn incense or sit in an uncomfortable position. The entire procedure is very straightforward and anyone can do it. All you need is somewhere private and quiet and approximately fifteen to twenty minutes of your time.

This technique is very valuable and extremely successful and I really urge you to try it if you are stressed. It relaxes you, but it also does much more than that. It brings about a wonderful feeling of peace, calm and stillness, both on a physical and on a mental level.

The technique is made up of a specially formulated routine of some of the Stress Cures contained in this section. As each Cure is performed, the degree of relaxation that you are able to attain is increased, so that by the end of the technique you will have totally let go of yourself. It can be used either on a regular basis, which I strongly recommend, or occasionally, when you are feeling particularly stressed.

### WHAT TO DO
Find somewhere quiet and private and sit comfortably cross-legged on the floor. If you need to support your back, lean it against a sturdy piece of furniture.

**4** Perform the Out-Breath Technique again, feeling the entire weight of the body sinking deeper and deeper into the ground with each out-breath.

This routine should take approximately fifteen minutes, after which time slowly straighten your back, shoulders and head. Wait another few moments and gradually open your eyes. Adjust to what you can see and then stand up and return to your everyday life, but try to stay quiet and relaxed.

**3** Perform the Neck Technique (*see page 52*).

# STRESS CURE B
## Stressful Life Situations and their Remedies

This section of the book is to do with the way we behave in stressful situations and how we can help ourselves to alleviate the stress.

There are many thousands of situations in which people feel stressed, and it would be impossible to cover them all here. So what I have done is to choose some of the more common ones that most people will be able to relate to.

These are then analysed and practical advice given. If your particular stress situation is not included, simply find the one that is closest in character to it and follow those instructions.

One of the biggest problems with stress is that we may know what we ought to do in the long-term either to reduce or remove it, but that doesn't help us on the spot, in our day-to-day lives. We need to know how to handle it when we are in that same stressful situation again.

These techniques and tips have been formulated to do just that and they can be used as a practical step-by-step guide. They will help to eliminate the physical, mental and emotional symptoms of your stress. When and if those symptoms return, you simply repeat the procedure.

You will see that the Stress Cures in this section are divided up into four main groups.

The first deals with situations that you may find yourself in at work; the second with some typical social and personal problems; the third with an assortment of very common life situations that can cause great anxiety; and the fourth includes some special tips for specific problems.

Do remember when you look at these behavioural examples that they are just that. The situations that I have described are unlikely to duplicate your experience exactly. That is not the intention. They are provided as a guide to show how you can alter your behaviour and your reactions in order to reduce or remove your stress, so be prepared to adapt them to apply to your own particular circumstances.

## A Word about Long-Term Stress

The Cures in both this and the other sections of the book can successfully relieve and remove the negative results of your stress, if necessary over and over again. However, if you have been suffering from a particular stress problem or problems for quite some time, those symptoms will keep on returning until you finally remove the *origin* of the stress. This may mean taking a very critical look at your life and then making some radical changes. You are the only one who can do this, but I believe that the use of the techniques in this book will go a long way to equipping and helping you.

# AT WORK

## JOB INTERVIEWS

When faced with this daunting task most of us go wobbly at the knees. We are literally on trial and we feel that it isn't just a case of whether we can do the actual job or not, but also how we look, sound and generally behave that will get us the job or not.

We become very self-conscious and tense for fear that we might do or say the wrong thing, sometimes even to the point that we practically stop breathing. Our bodies feel awkward and we get embarrassed. The interview may only take a few minutes but to us it can seem like hours. It is also one of those experiences that doesn't seem to get any easier or comfortable as you go through life. No matter what your age or how many times you do it, it always remains an ordeal.

The worst aspect of job interviews is the fact that your nervousness, anxiety and resultant inhibition prevent you from communicating your true worth to a potential employer; that is the most bitter pill of all to swallow. You get home and reflect on how you should have handled yourself in the interview, and how differently you would do it all if you had the chance again.

The object then is to prepare well, physically and mentally, for your interview, and to know how to let yourself go and relax once you get there so that you can give of your best. These tips are designed to help you do that and to make your next job interview less stressful.

## WHAT TO DO

**1** Dress extremely comfortably so that you don't find yourself fidgeting with your clothes. If you are unsure of what to wear, it is a good idea to select your clothes the night before. That way you won't give yourself the added pressure of having to make a snap decision on the actual day when you might be pushed for time.

**2** Don't eat heavily before the interview. It could either make you drowsy or, because of your tension, give you indigestion.

**3** You need to prepare before the actual interview by practising the following techniques: The Out-Breath Technique (*see page 30*). The Instant Relaxation for the Stomach Technique (*see page 60*), the technique for stress-free and relaxed sitting (*page 36*) and the Deviation of Focus Technique (*see page 34*). Do them several times until you feel completely familiar with them.

**4** On both the night before and the morning of your interview, try to execute the Deep Meditation Technique (*see page 68*) exactly as recommended.

**5** Try to arrive approximately five to eight minutes before your interview appointment. That will give you sufficient time to find the actual office or room that you will be interviewed in, to pop into the loo if you need to, and so on. It is not a good idea to arrive too early because you can become stressed while you are waiting. Whatever you do, however, don't be late. This not only gives the interviewer a bad first impression of you but it also creates a phenomenal amount of stress which means that you start off with a big handicap.

**6** When sitting and waiting to go into the interview room, adjust your physical position and lean back in your chair if you can, so that you are not holding any muscles unnecessarily tense. Then slow your breathing down by using the Out-Breath Technique.

**7** Do not think about what awaits you, but instead practise the Deviation of Focus Technique. By this time, you should only have a couple of minutes to wait.

**8** When you are asked to go in, don't immediately jump up in a panic. Take a few seconds to gather yourself together and to take a slow breath. Then get up in your own time and walk purposefully into the room.

**9** Sit where indicated and concentrate not on the interviewer but on putting yourself into a really comfortable position, ie, feet squarely on the ground and your back straight and as supported as possible.

**10** The position of your hands is very important, as they can convey much about your feelings. They need to be in a comfortable position where you will not be inclined to fidget. I find the following positions particularly good.

If there are arms on your chair, rest your elbows on them and interlock your fingers, making a pyramid with your two index fingers. Then simply look at your interviewer. This position communicates not only strength, but also that you are ready to commence. If the chair doesn't have arms, or if you prefer, you can simply relax the hands in your lap, either loosely interlocking the fingers or with the palms uppermost, one hand resting in the other. When you have decided where to put your hands, make sure that you also let your shoulders drop and relax.

**11** Do not feel obliged to say anything. Be prepared to wait until the interviewer begins. We always have a strong urge to 'make conversation' and to avoid

awkward silences, as we see them, but in the context of an interview, this can be a mistake. One is never quite sure what to say, and the words don't usually sound right. All that you may achieve is an increase in your stress.

**12** When you are asked the first question, don't feel that you have to race to answer it. Really think about it and consider exactly what you want to say. Then take a breath and calmly reply, thinking about each word and what it means as you are saying it. Don't wonder or worry what the interviewer may be thinking about you.

**13** If you don't know the answer to a question, or would like to have it repeated because you don't understand it, say so. Your honesty will be much more appreciated than if you pretend to know something that you don't.

**14** Handle each question as it comes in exactly the same way, really concentrating and listening to what you are being asked. By devoting your attention solely to what is actually going on, you will automatically cut out any pre-occupation with your own performance.

**15** If at any point during the interview you start to feel uncomfortable or stressed for any reason, immediately initiate the Out-Breath Technique and then return your attention to what is being said.

## MEETINGS WITH THE BOSS AND WITH COLLEAGUES

First of all let's look at why meetings with the boss can be so frightening. Some of us fear the worst when such a meeting is requested. We immediately think that we have made some mistake and are going to be reprimanded. Even when we go to routine and expected meetings with the boss, we imagine all sorts of non-existent problems and start to worry.

Our fear stems back to childhood when the authority figures in our lives – parents, teachers and so on – made us feel bad by telling us off

when we did something wrong. The boss too represents an authority figure and therefore we fear a repeat of our childhood experiences. This brings back unhappy and humiliating memories, many of which are unconscious, and we are simply aware of feeling bad and anxious somewhere inside ourselves. It is not a good sensation to know that somebody has the power to make us feel like naughty children, and the prospect of a meeting with the boss can in effect do this and consequently be very unsettling.

Of course, we know how ridiculous this seems. After all, we are grown up now. However, these are very real fears for many of us, and if this is something that truly stresses and worries you, then it can make you apprehensive and miserable but it doesn't have to be that way.

## Let's Look at Meetings Generally

These can be meetings with one or several people, and they too can be very stressful experiences. We are often afraid that at meetings with colleagues we might be shown up as incompetent and made to look a fool. This can lead to us being so inhibited that we perform badly to the extent of not getting our intended points across.

Then there can often be an element of competition at meetings, with people fighting to inflate their own egos. This can lead to us behaving or reacting in a wholly unnatural and stressful way.

## WHAT TO DO

**1** Prepare really well for your meeting, getting all the information that you might need to hand well in advance.

**2** If you have time, follow instructions 2, 3 & 4 of the previous Cure, so that your mind and body are in a relaxed, confident state.

**3** When the meeting begins, adjust your position so that you are not holding any muscles unneccessarily tense.

**4** If you are sitting at a desk or table, don't crouch over if you can possibly help it. Sit with your back well-supported.

**5** Using the Out-Breath and muscle relaxing techniques, try to concentrate on what is happening at the meeting and not on yourself.

**6** Before you speak, pause, always take a breath, and then speak really clearly and slowly without raising your voice.

**7** Try to resist any urge to interrupt, and make notes to remind yourself of any points that you wish to make later.

**8** If you find yourself becoming stressed or tense during the meeting, immediately instigate the Deviation of Focus Technique (*see page 34*).

---

## TAKING CRITICISM

We all find it very hard to take criticism. Our defences shoot up and we feel that we are being attacked.

Our usual reaction when we are criticized is an indignant one, and this applies whether or not we know the people or person well who is doing the criticizing.

Witness, for example, the usual reaction when one driver makes a derogatory comment to another about his or her driving. It is usually one of outrage and thoughts of: 'How dare they?'

## Why Does Criticism Make us Feel so Bad?

The reason is that when we are criticized we feel, wrongly, that we ourselves are being judged, not on the basis of what we have actually done or said, but on who we are as people. We feel this no matter what the actual reason for the criticism. The comments made to us could be of a totally non-personal nature, but we nevertheless feel personally offended and hurt by them. This is, of course, irrational but on an emotional and sometimes sub-conscious level, that is how we feel.

Criticism also stops us in our tracks and shocks us. We are lulled by a sense of security because our society is one in which most people go out of their way to be nice and polite to each other. We are, therefore, unprepared and stunned when suddenly those same people appear to change and are openly critical of us.

As a rule, most of us are pretty confident that we can successfully hide our very worst 'faults' from the world. These are the character traits that we regard as defects in our own personalities. However, when we are criticized, we are thrown into a sort of panic because we think that our cover is blown and that our deepest inadequacies have been exposed. We feel small, vulnerable and ashamed and our sense of security crumbles around us.

The most important thing to learn in handling criticism is how to differentiate between a valid comment made by somebody about something that we might have done or said, and a personal attack that is specifically designed to hurt us. We can then judge the criticism for what it really is and treat it accordingly.

In our day-to-day social exchanges, jobs and personal relationships, there are inevitably going to be occasions when other people criticize us. We can't avoid it, but we can learn how best to handle it without it causing us too much stress.

## WHAT TO DO

**1** The first thing to do when you are being criticized is to listen carefully and concentrate on what is being said. That means registering every word so that you can remember as much of it as possible.

**2** Think about your breathing and try to remember to take a deep breath before you reply.

**3** Even if you are fuming and feel that the criticism is unfair, try not to react instantly to it with outrage. You need time to cool down and to think about what was said, so say something like 'That's interesting, I'd like to think about what you said' or 'I'd like some time to consider that'.

**4** You will then have given yourself the opportunity to do just that, think about it. Think about the actual words that were used in the criticism and see if they truly relate to what you have done or said, or whether you consider the comments to be unfair. It can help your analysis of the criticism at this stage if you jot your thoughts down on paper.

**5** If, after objective examination, you feel the criticism to be unjustified, tell the person exactly what you think but taking care not to do it in an aggressive way. You can say something like 'I'd really like to talk to you about your comments the other day'. Or, 'I've been thinking about what you said and I don't agree because....' Conversely, if you decide that the criticism was possibly valid, tell the person so. Honest exchange usually makes for better relationships all round, whether they be business or personal.

**6** If you decide that the criticism was an unjust personal attack on you, it is fine to be assertive and say so. There are various ways of putting it, but something like 'I would like you to know that I regard your comments as unfortunate and untrue'. Or, 'I'd like you to know that I think your criticism has no real foundation, but it's interesting that you feel a need to make a remark of that type to me'.

If you were hurt by the remark, then it is fine to tell the criticiser that too. There will always, unfortunately, be people who try to bolster their own insecurity by putting other people down and criticizing them. If you feel that this is the case, you don't have to let people get away with it at your expense. Saying what you actually feel will be a tremendous boost to you, both in terms of status and self-respect, and will also gain you the admiration and respect of the person unjustly criticizing you.

**7** When we are criticized, an immediate reaction is for us to tense up physically, so try the next time it happens to consciously let go of all unnecessary muscles. To help you to do this, practise the Body Check (*see page 66*).

**8** Be aware of your breathing and don't allow it to quicken up, which it will tend to do if you become stressed. If you feel this happening, execute the Out-Breath Technique (*see page 30*) and this will immediately relax you. Also, remember the breathing rule when you are talking to somebody and feeling stressed: always take a deep, smooth breath before you speak.

---

# GIVING CRITICISM

When we have to criticize somebody and we feel uncomfortable about it, we can become stressed and go about things in the wrong way. The result is that we can be too aggressive or too soft, and so we can create bad feeling or fail to get our message across.

The latter happens because most of us, having been on the painful, receiving end of criticism, try to avoid having to hurt other people in the same way. Our concern means that we end up not communicating as clearly as we should, which causes confusion for the person taking the criticism and dissatisfaction for the person giving it.

The other extreme is for us to be too hard. This can happen when we are afraid that we might not make our point clearly enough, and we become emphatic and overbearing.

## *WHAT TO DO*

**1** Resist any temptation to practise or rehearse what you are going to say in advance, or how you are going to say it. It doesn't usually work. Also, don't imagine what the other person's reactions to your comments might be. People are unpredictable.
**2** It helps to turn the occasion into a two-way conversation, rather than you talking at the person or making a speech, because that always feels intimidating to the other person. Therefore, invite the person to be part of the proceedings by saying something like 'I'd like your opinion of this piece of work, this project, this situation that we've got ourselves into'. Or, if it is appropriate, something like 'Are there problems about you getting in on time in the mornings and can we talk about it?'. Always try to use these sorts of involving phrases. It conveys the message that you have some regard and respect for the other person and are interested in their views.

Also, be honest when you find it difficult to tell somebody something. Say 'Frankly, I find it really hard to say this, but...'. Most people will relax if they feel that you are not out to get them.
**3** If you are nervous, take a breath before you speak, and try to modulate your voice so that it is clear but not loud.
**4** Really look at the person that you are with and be aware of their reactions to what you are saying.
**5** Allow time in the conversation for them to think and then reply to your queries. Try not to interrupt or hurry them.
**6** At the end of your conversation, if you are in any doubt that you have not communicated the crucial points, ask the other person what they found of value in the conversation. Their reply should indicate whether or not they have received and understood the intended messages.
**7** You are in a position of power when you are criticizing others and it is easy to abuse that power for your own ends. Be careful that this doesn't happen and try to be pleasant and fair without being patronizing. That way you stand a good chance not only of your criticism being accepted and acted upon, but also of your relationship with the person being greatly improved.

# TALKING ON THE PHONE

Most of us regard the telephone as nothing more than a convenient way of communicating with others and just a normal part of everyday life. However to some people it can be a daunting experience and a great source of stress.

Since we can't be seen, our voices literally represent us when we are on the phone and people are judging us totally by how we sound. We can subsequently become concerned at how we are coming across and feel that we must make an effort to be perceived in the way that we want. It is then that we can become obsessed with our own performance. We ask ourselves such questions as:

Do we sound confident enough?

Are we speaking too loudly or too softly?

Are there too many awkward silences?

Does the person on the other end know that I am afraid?

The result is that instead of concentrating on the actual exchange that is taking place, our minds become absorbed by these other pre-occupations. Ironically, we can then end up by achieving exactly what we dread, namely giving a wrong or a bad impression of ourselves.

Try the following tips if you get stressed or nervous when you have either to make or take telephone calls.

## WHAT TO DO

**1** When you use the telephone, try to put yourself into a physically relaxed position. If you are sitting, try to lean back and support your back. Then do the Body Check (*see page 66*) and let go of any muscles that you are gripping unnecessarily. This is particularly relevant to your grip on the receiver.

**2** If you are making the call, practise the Out-Breath Technique (*see page 30*) a few times to relax yourself before you begin.

**3** I always think it helps in reducing stress when using the telephone if you have a pen and pad handy. This will allow you to jot down what you want to say in advance, and to remember any points made during the conversation. Having something to do with your hands like this is also very effective in taking your mind off yourself.

**4** Always take a deep, smooth breath before you speak, and speak slowly and clearly, concentrating on every word. When the other person speaks, concentrate solely on what they are saying.

**5** Never rush to answer the phone if you can help it, although it is automatic for most of us to do this. Try, if you can, to allow it to ring *AT LEAST* four times, even if you are sitting right beside it. The caller will not usually ring off after such a short time and these few moments can be very valuable for you to prepare and relax yourself.

On the first ring, you stop whatever else you are doing and simply register that the phone has rung. Don't do anything else.

On the second ring, move into a comfortable position.

On the third ring, concentrate on breathing slowly and deeply.

On the fourth ring you are perfectly ready to pick up the phone and speak calmly.

If you are not near the phone when it rings, allow an extra two or three rings to get there without rushing. Then proceed as above.

**6** Don't interrupt the other person. This will just make them nervous too. Wait until you are sure that they have finished speaking, think about what you want to say, then take a breath and speak. It doesn't matter at all if this means that there are occasional silences. This is far better than the stress of both people trying to talk at the same time.

**7** If you get nervous on the phone, you may often find that you finish the call not only tense but also dissatisfied because you haven't said the things that you really intended to say. If this is the case, you can prepare by writing these things down beforehand and, at the beginning of the conversation, tell the other person that you have several points that you'd like to make, and go through them one at a time.

That way, you have warned the person in advance and you will be less likely to feel pressured because you think you are taking up too much of their time.
**8** If, in the course of the conversation, you feel yourself becoming tense or nervous, do a quick Body Check to see if you are leaning forward or gripping any muscles that aren't needed. If you are, alter your position to a more relaxed one and let the muscles go. Then execute the Out-Breath Technique a few times.

## MAKING A SPEECH

Many of us have to make a speech at some time in our lives, often in the course of our jobs. Without doubt, it can be one of the most terrifying experiences we may ever have to put ourselves through.

Repeating the ordeal doesn't appear to make it any easier either because, if that were true, professional actors and other performers would be perfectly at home having to appear regularly in front of an audience. In fact, the reverse is usually true and they are petrified each and every time they have to do it. This is just one of the many reasons that show business can be such a stressful occupation.

There are a few people who appear to be able to make speeches calmly, confidently and at ease, but you will generally find that this is something that they have had to put a bit of work into. It rarely, if ever, comes naturally.

Although you may start off extremely stressed and tense at the prospect of making a speech, it is possible both to reduce and to eliminate the stress and to make your speech in a relaxed and confident way. It may even be possible, believe it or not, to actually enjoy the experience.

Generally, you will know well in advance if you are required to make a speech, and this advance warning is good because you will need time to prepare.

## WHAT TO DO

**1** Practise the following techniques regularly until you are comfortable and familiar with them during the days or even weeks leading up to your speech.
- Out-Breath Technique (*see page 30*).
- Arms, Hands and Fingers (*see page 58*).
- Buttocks (*see page 62*).
- Stomach (*see page 60*).
- Total Relaxation with Mind-Clearing Technique (*see page 46*).
- Deep Meditation (*see page 68*).
- Body Check (*see page 66*).

Learning these techniques will help you, on the day of your speech, to release any unnecessarily tense muscles and to slow your breathing down, both of which you need in order to relax.

**2** Find out exactly where and how you will be delivering your speech. You need to know the size and shape of the room or hall; whether there is a stage or platform; if you will be required to use a microphone or not; exactly how long you are expected to speak; whether there will be somewhere to put your notes if you have any, and any other queries you may have.

**3** Do your homework thoroughly in terms of gathering and studying any necessary data, so that when you come to make your speech, you either have the facts in your head or to hand.

**4** The evening before your speech, practise the Deep Meditation Technique followed by the Total Relaxation with Mind-Clearing Technique.

## On the Actual Day of the Speech

**5** Try to practise one or both of the techniques mentioned in **4**, depending on how much time you have available.

**6** Eat and drink lightly and, whatever you do, don't be tempted to have an alcoholic drink or two to give you 'Dutch courage'. It usually doesn't work and it can have disastrous results.

**7** Dress comfortably and especially avoid wearing clothes that are tight around the waist or neck.

**8** Try to spend the final few minutes before making your speech quietly on your own. This gives you an opportunity either to check your notes or just to think about the points that you want to make. If you are feeling nervous or tense, execute the Out-Breath Technique a few times.

**9** When you are announced or it is time to begin, take a deep breath and then walk purposefully to your destination, not looking to the left or right of you, but to where you are going.

**10** When you reach your place, take a few moments to organize yourself. There is no great rush. If you have notes, or other reference material, put them down carefully where you will have easy access to them. Then turn your attention to getting comfortable.

**11** Stand with your feet about twelve to fifteen inches apart and your weight evenly distributed. Do a quick body check and release any muscles held unnecessarily tense.

**12** Now, simply spend the next few moments taking in and familiarizing yourself with what you can see. Let your eyes wander around the room. Notice any familiar faces. Roughly how many people there are. The colour of the curtains, and so on. This may seem silly, but it will help to take away any last-minute panic by taking your mind off yourself.

The last three points may sound as though you need a lot of time before you actually begin to speak: but in fact only a few moments will have elapsed since you walked onto the stage.

**13** Now you are ready to begin. Think of what you want to say. Take a deep breath and start.

**14** Concentrate totally on the meaning of each word and whether your audience can easily understand what you are saying. The more you think about what your audience is getting from you in terms of clear information, the less you will be concerned with your own performance. Taking the trouble to pick out and really look at some of the faces in the crowd will help you, because you will be able to see if they are confused, bored or interested. The audience will also feel that you are talking 'to' them and not 'at' them.

**15** Don't be afraid to stop if you need a moment, either to look at your notes or simply to think about what you want to say next. So many people feel that it is a crime to stop during a speech, but why should it be? After all, you are not trying to be impossibly perfect, but simply to impart information efficiently, and if you are casual and relaxed, so will your audience be. There is nothing worse than somebody giving a speech as though they have a train to catch. It makes the audience feel very cheated.

**16** As soon as you feel any signs of nervousness returning, do an immediate body check. Release any gripped muscles that you don't need, paying particular attention to your shoulders and stomach. Then concentrate on your breathing. Slow it down if you can by doing even one slow Out-Breath, and take a deep breath in again before you speak. Then concentrate once more purely on the meaning of your words.

**17** At the end of your speech, take the time to look at and sincerely thank the audience for their attention. Gather your things calmly together and walk off the stage.

## ADDRESSING A SMALL GROUP

Many of the tips in the previous section also apply to this sometimes stressful experience, but there are differences. For example, addressing a small group of colleagues, friends or contemporaries can be nerve-racking because, unlike when making a speech, you are in much more intimate contact with the people around you and, therefore, much more aware of their reactions to you.

You are also very accessible when addressing a small group, and people will often feel entitled to interrupt and question the validity of what you are saying. It is important therefore to be absolutely sure of your ground and to work out carefully in advance what you want to say and how you want to say it.

## WHAT TO DO

1 Think ahead about the room in which you will be addressing the group. How large is it? Will everybody be sitting or standing, or will it just be you that is standing?

2 Your body language will communicate much about how you are feeling at such close quarters, so you need to be able to relax instantly if and when you physically tense up. You will help yourself considerably if for several days, or even weeks, before your talk, you practise the following techniques regularly.
- Out-Breath Technique (see page 30).
- Arms, Hands and Fingers (see page 58).
- Neck (see page 52).
- Shoulders (see page 56).
- Stomach (see page 60).
- Sitting (see page 36).
(This final technique will be particularly valuable in ensuring that you are stress-free and relaxed if you are sitting down to give your talk).

3 On the day that you give your talk, as near to the appointed hour as possible, try to find somewhere quiet where you can be alone for a few minutes. Practise the Out-Breath Technique, and both the Shoulder and Stomach relaxation techniques if you can.

Then follow the advice given under *Making a Speech* beginning at point 6 (see page 77), adapting it slightly to fit your situation if necessary.

## BUSINESS LUNCHES AND DINNERS

Eating is supposed to be a relaxed and enjoyable experience. However, when it is connected with business, it can be anything but. The business lunch or dinner can turn into a dreaded duty and can lead to all sorts of stress-related conditions.

The problem with such occasions is the fact that people are rarely relaxed. Their minds are often focused on things such as the impression that they are making, or how they can best realize their own objectives. These preoccupations swim around in their heads, and this can cause considerable strain and tension.

Another reason that business lunches or dinners are so stressful is that you can suddenly find yourself sitting very close to someone that you don't know very well, and with whom, up until now, you have had a very formal relationship. The majority of these mealtime meetings take place in restaurants where the tables tend to be rather small; you may feel uncomfortably trapped in a rather physically intimate situation which can be intimidating and cause you to feel embarrassed and self-conscious. If you are sitting in a cramped, unnaturally tense position, this also sets up stress which may be felt particularly in the shoulder and neck areas.

The stress of these occasions can also cause us to grip our stomach muscles and, if we do this when we are actually eating, it interferes with the digestive processes and can cause painful and unpleasant conditions to develop. We are also likely to bolt our food, allowing insufficient time to chew it, and mastication is essential for good digestion. We do this out of a nervous concern that we must be ready to speak as soon as the other person stops, thereby avoiding any 'awkward' pauses. Laughing nervously when you think you should, rather than when something is genuinely funny, is a common occurrence and is not only stressful but can also cause rather a lot of air to be swallowed. This in turn can create uncomfortable wind.

Drinking too much alcohol is a hazard of business lunches or dinners and is best avoided, as its effects on your judgement and behaviour could work to your disadvantage.

If you experience stress on these occasions the following tips should help to make them less of an ordeal in the future. They will also help you to avoid some of the common and unpleasant conditions that can be the result of this type of stress and tension.

## WHAT TO DO

1 Much of your stress reduction depends upon your physical position and subsequent relaxation. Once in the restaurant, sit well back in your seat, legs apart, feet planted solidly on the floor.
2 Let your shoulders drop and relax and put your

hands where they too can relax and where you won't fidget. For example, let them rest in your lap.
3 If you feel nervous or tense, practise the Out-Breath Technique (see page 30). It is possible to execute a subtle version of this technique that won't be noticeable to other people.
4 Take only small mouthfuls of food and chew well before swallowing.
5 Don't eat and talk at the same time. A few moments of silence will not be disastrous and the pause, allowing attention to be turned to the food, could well be appreciated by the other person.
6 Pay special attention to your stomach muscles and do periodic checks to see if you are gripping them. If you are, let them go.
7 The same applies to your shoulders. If the muscles are held tense, release them.
8 From time to time, put your knife and fork down between mouthfuls, and lean back in your seat and relax. Try to breathe slowly.
9 Always take a breath before you speak and try not to rush what you have to say.
10 If you feel yourself becoming nervous and awkward, repeat the Out-Breath Technique as before a few times, and couple it with the Deviation of Focus Technique (see page 34).
11 Lastly, it may help to know that your companion is quite likely to be as nervous and tense as you are, so spare a sympathetic thought for him or her and appreciate that you probably share the same feelings.

## TRAVELLING TO AND FROM WORK

No matter what mode of transport you use, getting to and from work can be very stressful. Having to travel on exactly the same route, at the same time, day after day, is a monotonous experience and something that just has to be got through.

The boredom that seems endemic to commuting can itself be a powerful source of

stress. It can cause strong but suppressed feelings of resentment because you are forced to go through the same ritual day after day. That resentment can be turned in on yourself and stress and tension can be the result. Another common reaction when one is suppressing resentment is to launch an unjust, verbal attack on anyone who happens to be nearby. This usually has nothing whatever to do with what that person might have actually said or done; it is simply because you need something or somebody on whom to vent your frustration and that person is conveniently close.

Different ways of travelling carry with them their own particular stresses. Commuting by train or bus, for example, can be stressful because you are forced to be physically close to total strangers without making any 'real' verbal or mental contact with them. This can be disturbing because we are all used to having a certain amount of 'personal' physical space around us. When we are deprived of this space we can feel invaded, vulnerable and insecure. We then psychologically shrink into ourselves for self-protection and cut ourselves off from our surroundings as much as we can. By doing this we are creating the emotional contradiction that we are with people but trying to be alone. This can build up considerable stress levels inside us.

Driving to work is intrinsically stressful and elsewhere you will find advice and tips to help you to deal with this (*see page 40*). Compared to public transport, driving has advantages and disadvantages. One of the advantages is that it allows you to travel, to a large extent, in privacy and in an environment of your own choosing. A disadvantage is the fact that it is impossible to relax completely while driving, whereas there is a possibility of this happening on public transport.

Whatever way you travel, stress can be an extremely unpleasant and unwelcome part of it. If this is the case for you, try to reduce or even eliminate your stress by using some of the following tips.

## WHAT TO DO

**1** If you use public transport, try to use your travelling time to do something interesting or constructive. For example, there may be a particular subject, language or hobby that you have always wanted to study or learn about but have never had the time. Alternatively, you could make lists of things to be done or that you would like to do in the future. If you choose to read, pick something stimulating and worthwhile.

**2** Try to make contact with one or more of your travelling companions. Start up a light-hearted conversation one day. You might be pleasantly surprised at how interesting and rewarding such a relationship can become.

**3** If neither of the above suggestions appeals to you, travelling gives you a wonderful opportunity to rest your mind by daydreaming. Close your eyes and just let your mind wander. Dwell on pleasant memories, dream about the things you would like to have or experience in the future.

**4** Try to get as physically comfortable as you can. If you are lucky enough to get a seat have your legs uncrossed and your feet squarely on the floor. Sit right back in your seat with your back supported and relax your shoulders, arms and hands. If you are forced to stand, have your weight evenly distributed and consciously let go of any muscles held unnecessarily tense.

**5** Breathe deeply and slowly using the Out-Breath Technique (*see page 30*) and repeat several times if and when you feel yourself becoming stressed, irritated or annoyed.

**6** Stagger your travelling times if at all possible, so that one or both of your daily journeys is outside the rush hour.

**7** When you get home at night, before you eat, try to get into the habit of practising Deep Meditation and the Total Relaxation with Mind-Clearing Techniques (*see pages 68 and 46 respectively*).

# AT LEISURE

## MEETING NEW PEOPLE

Meeting people for the first time can be worrying and stressful for many of us. We regard meeting new people as a risky business. After all, they don't owe us anything and they don't, therefore, have to be polite and 'nice' to us, as is usually the case with established relationships. So we worry and wonder what impression we are making on them and look anxiously for any signs that might indicate approval or disapproval.

For most of us, this strong need for acceptance exists because we are never quite sure of our true value. Therefore, when a stranger's manner shows that we are acceptable, it boosts our self-confidence and self-esteem. Our logic says: 'Well, that person thinks that I'm O.K., so I must be'.

The problem is that our need for acceptance can be so intense that, when we meet new people, our thoughts are almost exclusively devoted to this need. We can be so taken up with ourselves that we don't truly experience what the other people are like. This is a pity, because many great opportunities to really get to know people and to begin enjoyable and enriching relationships can be lost in this way.

Conversely, our tension and nervousness prevent the 'new' people that we are meeting from getting an accurate impression of how we really are. Our anxiety for approval creates such stress that we end up being too nervous to be ourselves.

The preoccupation with how we are coming across can turn the experience of meeting new people into an absolute agony which many people try to avoid. It is, however, necessary from time to time unless we are prepared severely to limit our social lives.

The following tips should help you not only to reduce and remove the stress from meeting new people, but actually to enjoy and appreciate the experience.

### WHAT TO DO

**1** Try not to think at all beforehand about the people you are going to meet. That means don't think about how they will look, how they will be dressed, what they will think of you, and so on. Every time you find yourself having such thoughts, wrench your mind away and concentrate completely on something entirely different. You will find the Quick Meditation Technique (*see page 67*) particularly helpful in this respect.

**2** When you are introduced to new people, try not to glance at them and immediately look away, even though this is a typical nervous reaction. It will help you considerably if you make yourself concentrate on them for a few moments. People usually feel rather flattered if you do this because it shows that you are taking a genuine interest in them. Look at their eyes, face, hair and so on. If you concentrate totally, there won't be any room inside your mind to be worried about yourself. To help you with this, practise the Deviation of Focus Technique (*page 34*).

**3** It will greatly increase your confidence if you are physically relaxed and comfortable, so try to stand in a very solid position with your feet planted squarely on the ground and your weight evenly distributed. Then do a Body Check (*see page 66*) to see if you are gripping any muscles unnecessarily and, if this is the case, let them go.

**4** If you feel nervous, try to slow your breathing down by using the Out-Breath Technique (*see page 30*) and, before you speak, always take a smooth, deep breath.

**5** Don't feel that you are in any way in competition with these people, because you aren't. Tell yourself that there is only one of you in the whole world and that you are unique. This is true, for nobody has precisely your ideas, your imagination, your taste, your feelings, your looks.

**6** Try to take a positive approach. If you are in a situation where circumstances lead you to meet new people, why not resolve to get the most that you possibly can out of the experience? After all, this exact situation with these people is a 'one off' and will never happen again. That doesn't mean that you have to like everyone that you meet. We can't like everyone. What you *can* usually do, though, if you take the trouble to look, is to find something that genuinely interests you about most people. That may mean asking a few questions and drawing the person out of their shell a bit if they are shy, but the effort can be well worth it. You may be surprised at how quickly you can forget all about yourself, relax, and start to enjoy the experience, once you become absorbed in the other person.

**7** Lastly, take heart from the fact that the vast majority of people feel exactly as you do. Actually being able to tell the other person or people how you feel can be very effective in immediately breaking the ice and establishing a sympathetic rapport. For example, you could say something like, 'It's ridiculous, I know, but I actually feel quite nervous at meeting you.' Or 'It's funny, but I get really scared when I meet new people. Does that ever happen to you?'

***Note:*** See also *Going to a Party* (*page 85*).

## GOING ON A DATE

A date with someone whom you think is a bit special is more stressful than perhaps any other social occasion. You are aware, at the back of your mind, that if it turns out to be the right person, the date could literally change your life.

The feeling of being on trial, and of having only this one chance to make your impact, sets up stresses that are similar in some ways to those of a job interview. Surprising as it may seem, the two situations do have quite a bit in common, as do both the strategy you should adopt and the way you should prepare for it.

You are anxious to give the other person a good impression of yourself and you therefore put a lot of effort into being charming, amusing, considerate, intelligent, confident, polite and anything else that you think the other person will like and be attracted to. At the same time, you are concerned not to appear too eager. Of course, the keener you are on the other person, the harder you try. You daren't relax because you are afraid that, if you do, you may lapse back into being your normal self and reveal your shortcomings – as you see them – whereupon your date will immediately lose interest in you.

The effort needed to sustain this near 'perfect' image is tremendous, and it consequently creates an enormous amount of stress. This tension, coupled with self-absorption regarding your own behaviour, can result in your mind and your energy being totally taken up with it. This means that you have nothing left with which to assess or truly experience the other person or, indeed, the date itself. And by allowing your stress to take over, far from presenting yourself at your best, you may well put the person off by your abnormal, tense and exaggerated behaviour. You are then left wondering what might have been had you acted differently or been able to be more your normal self. An all-too-common situation and one that need never happen.

Although we won't often admit it, either to ourselves or to others, a lot of our hopes and dreams can be pinned on a date, and even more so when it is a first date. In order to handle it as well as we can, we need to be able to be ourselves and to relax, This applies not only on the actual date itself, but also beforehand, when our anticipation can cause a lot of nervousness.

These tips are designed to help you to relax and to enable you to remove the stress and the tension from your dates in the future.

## WHAT TO DO

1 Before your date, whether you have days, weeks or even longer to wait, begin to practise the following techniques.

- Out-Breath Technique (*see page 30*).
- Deviation of Focus Technique (*page 34*).
- Face (*see page 50*).
- Shoulders (*page 56*).
- Arms, Hands and Fingers (*see page 58*).
- Stomach (*see page 60*).
- Body Check (*see page 66*).

These techniques will relax you generally as well as in the specific areas of the body that tend to tense up when you are nervous. They will, therefore, not only relax you in advance of your date but also be an invaluable aid to 'letting go' on the actual date itself.

2 Dress very comfortably for your date in YOUR favourite clothes and don't speculate as to what clothes he or she would like to see you in. By wearing what you feel good in, you won't have to devote unnecessary time and attention to your appearance on the actual date. This will not only contribute to your overall relaxation, but it will also mean that you can devote more time and attention to the person that you are with.

3 Try, when you are getting ready or waiting for your date, to think about the other person, rather than about yourself. Think, for example, about the things that you already know about them and list them in your mind. Then concentrate on the things that you would like to know and decide which of them you might ask him or her about first. However, it is important that your desire to know about the other person is genuine. It will very quickly become obvious if you aren't really interested, and the other person will feel rejected and hurt. If you think hard, you will be able to come up with several 'real' questions. After all, you must have found this person interesting in order to be having a date with them in the first place.

4 Once you are on your date, be prepared to do a lot of listening. This will convey very strongly to the other person that you care more about what they are saying than your need to sell yourself by talking a lot. This will not only be taken as a compliment but will also make them feel comfortable and relaxed with you. It is neither desirable nor necessary to 'perform' brilliantly in order to impress people with one's personality. In fact, it usually does the opposite and puts people off. It is not only exhausting to be with someone 'presenting' themselves in this way, but it also exposes how insecure they are.

5 Try not to interrupt if you can possibly help it. The other person is probably nervous too and will assume that what he or she is saying is not interesting.

6 Try to concentrate on the person's face when they are talking to you or you to them. If you look away, it can communicate the message that you are bored, so even though you may be doing it out of nervousness, try to avoid it.

7 Whether you are sitting, standing or walking, if you begin to feel nervous or tense, immediately do a body check and release any muscles held unnecessarily tense.

8 Think about your breathing and, before you speak, take a slow, deep breath. If you feel your breathing quickening up, execute the Out-Breath Technique a few times.

9 Lastly, you will get the most from your date in terms of enjoyment, pleasure and satisfaction if you simply experience each moment as it happens, without worrying about what he or she thinks of you, what it all means, or whether you will see each other again. There will be time for all that later, so try not to be preoccupied with these thoughts on the date itself.

# GOING TO A PARTY

Theoretically, we should all love going to parties. After all, parties are designed for people to get together and have a great time.

We are *supposed* to enjoy ourselves and be happy and carefree, but more often than not we are scared, anxious, and painfully embarrassed. It feels to us much more like an endurance test than an enjoyable experience and we wonder why on earth we came. We resolve that each party will be our last but it rarely is, since most of us have an innate desire to be with other people and we always hope that the next one will be better.

Why do such carefully planned social gatherings so often turn out to be the agonizing occasions that they are for so many people?

Well, for a start, everyone knows that they will be expected both to be and, more importantly, to look 'happy' and so we all prepare ourselves to smile and laugh no matter what we may be feeling inside. This puts us under extreme strain because we are trying to achieve the impossible. Nobody can smile, laugh or be happy on cue because these are entirely spontaneous reactions. If you don't feel it, you can't 'be' it. So there we are, at the party, superficial smiles on our faces, feeling bad because we know we are being false, and our self-esteem and confidence are consequently diminishing. What makes things even worse is the fact that we suspect that the people around us know that we are pretending. They usually do, since they are playing the same game, but that doesn't make us feel any better.

Then there is the standard code of socially accepted behaviour at parties that we feel we have to conform to. This demands that we make 'nice, pleasant, polite' conversation. This, too, is a great strain, because we are feigning interest in conversations, saying things like 'Oh! how interesting' and 'Do tell me about so and so',

when we and the people we are with truly couldn't care less.

There is also often an element of competition at parties. People try desperately hard to impress one another with what they say or how they look, or who they have come to the party with, and so on. This is a strain both to participate in and to witness.

Probably the most terrifying thing about parties is the fact that our bodies can't and don't lie about what we are feeling. In spite of our efforts to hide and control our stress, terror, nervousness and embarrassment, our physical reactions reveal the truth. We then add substantially to our stress as we try to hide or mask these reactions. This is an example of what can happen.

Somebody looks at us and we begin to feel self-conscious about our appearance. We compare ourselves to the other people around us and decide that we are inadequate and inferior and that we would like to disappear into the ground. Our muscles tighten, ready for action, but we don't go anywhere, so the tension stays inside us. We try very hard to pretend to the outside world that we are really calm and relaxed, but the effort required to do this creates more strain, making things even worse. This is when we can start to feel hot and sweaty. The heart begins to race, the breathing to quicken up, and so on.

I sometimes wish that it were possible for somebody to blow a whistle at parties, as a signal for everybody to relax and be themselves. You would probably see the false smiles drop along with the hunched and tense shoulders, but the relief would be tremendous and there would be a real chance for satisfying communication to take place.

Having said how stressful parties are for most people, it doesn't have to be that way. You have the power to change things very much for the better, and to start to get some real value and enjoyment out of them.

## WHAT TO DO

**1** You will usually know well in advance when you are going to a party, and this gives you the chance to prepare really well. Practise the following techniques as often as you like. They will not only relax you generally, but also teach you how to relax specific parts of your mind and body when at the party.

- Out-Breath Technique (*see page 30*).
- Deviation of Focus Technique (*see page 34*).
- Shoulders (*see page 56*).
- Stomach (*see page 60*).
- Buttocks (*see page 62*).
- Body Check (*see page 66*).

**2** Most people like to wear special clothes for parties, but try to select clothes that you are really mentally and physically comfortable in. If you are often nervous about your appearance, it is a good idea to experiment and decide what to wear well before the day of the party.

**3** The journey to the party can often be very tense and stressful because you anticipate how terrible it is going to be. Try, if you can, to think about some positive points. For example, the food is usually good and special at parties, so go there with an appetite and plan to enjoy the spread. Tell yourself that there is probably going to be at least one person there of some interest to you and resolve to try to find him or her. If you know the host or hostess, think about and list in your head the things that you either like or don't like about them and do the same with the house or flat that the party is going to be held in. These and similar thoughts are designed to take your mind off yourself, so really concentrate on them.

**4** When you arrive at your destination, try to take a few moments to collect yourself and relax before you go in. Do this by executing the Out-Breath Technique a few times, and do a Body Check to see if you are holding any muscles unnecessarily tense. If you are, let them go.

**5** Once at the party, concentrate on what you find there, how the people and the place look and sound. Avoid thinking about yourself but, if this happens, concentrate hard on something outside yourself each time. The Deviation of Focus Technique that you have been practising will greatly help you in this type of situation.

**6** Look around, and decide if you would like to talk to somebody who genuinely takes your interest. Then try to go over and start up a conversation. Try not to feel obliged to talk to the person nearest you out of a sense of panic that you must be seen to be socializing from the moment that you arrive. It is perfectly alright to stand and take in the scene for a few moments. Don't worry what the other people around you might think – they are probably so involved with their own anxiety and nerves that their minds are on themselves.

**7** When you are having a conversation with someone, concentrate on what is being said, even though there may be a lot of noise going on around you. Don't feel that you have to smile and laugh, but simply ask the things that you genuinely want to know and then listen carefully to the answers. If you do this, you will react naturally, relax both yourself and the other person and enjoy the conversation.

**8** Should you feel yourself tensing up physically at any time, a quick Body Check will tell you which muscles you are gripping unnecessarily and you can let them go.

**9** If you feel yourself getting nervous, immediately perform the Out-Breath Technique and the Deviation of Focus Technique. Practise them for a few moments, then concentrate once again on the people or person that you are with. You can repeat this procedure during the party as often as you like.

**10** Lastly, try to remember that since you have made an effort to come to the party, you may as well try to get something out of it. Concentrate, therefore, on seeking out and finding things of real interest to you, rather than dwelling on your own feelings and thoughts.

***Note:*** See also *Meeting New People (page 82)*.

# ENTERTAINING AT HOME

Having people over to our homes and feeding and entertaining them is, we feel, a real test of our domestic and social skills. We are concerned, therefore, to make things as perfect as possible, and that means that we worry a lot. We worry about our homes and whether they look good, tidy, well furnished and smart enough. Likewise, is our cooking sophisticated or grand enough? Do we look alright ourselves and, once the guests arrive, are we able to entertain them properly?

We can be so insecure about home entertaining that when we come to do it, instead of it being a pleasant social occasion, it becomes an ordeal. Our guests, sensing our tension and nervousness, inevitably get sucked into the atmosphere and they too become stressed. The result is a tense, nervous group of people all trying desperately hard, without success, to relax and enjoy themselves. The evening is exhausting and we are left feeling flat, empty and depressed because we have failed to give our friends a good time.

Entertaining at home, however, can and should be a stress-free, relaxed and enjoyable experience. With a little bit of forward planning and thought, that is exactly what it can be.

## WHAT TO DO

I You are presumably inviting people that you like and who like you to your home, and this is why they are coming. Tell yourself this, and that your friends are not coming to judge your home, your cooking, or your professional entertaining skills.

2 If you are nervous, keep things very simple. That means choosing a dish or a menu that you have tried and tested many times before and feel very confident with. The food doesn't have to be so different from your everyday diet. I know of many highly successful occasions where baked beans on toast or the like have been enjoyed and a great time had by all.

3 Prepare as much in advance as you can so that you have very little to do when your guests arrive and will be able to sit down and relax and enjoy being with them. Otherwise you will be forever disappearing into the kitchen, never able really to participate in the conversation.

4 Entertaining in your own home gives you licence to wear whatever you like, so pick the most comfortable thing that you own.

5 If you feel tense before your guests arrive, go through the Deep Meditation Technique (see page 68). Then do the Total Relaxation with Mind-Clearing Technique (see page 46). You should allow yourself approximately forty minutes in total to perform both of these techniques slowly.

6 When it is time to eat, make sure that you enjoy both the food and the company. That, after all, is the whole point of the occasion. So often the person hosting the evening feels as though they are not part of the proceedings at all, so involved and engrossed are they in cooking, preparing and serving the food and worrying that everything is going well.

7 Relax both yourself and your guests by not rushing the meal. Sit back in your seat between mouthfuls and really taste and enjoy the food and the conversation.

8 Should you feel yourself getting tense at any point, slow your breathing down by practising the Out-Breath Technique (see page 30) and always take a long, slow, deep breath before you speak. Also, do a Body Check (see page 66) to see that you are not gripping any muscles that you don't need to, especially your shoulder and stomach muscles.

9 If you are intent on having a really good time yourself and you devote your mind and energy to this, then that is what will very probably happen. So relax, let go and enjoy yourself.

# A FORMAL FUNCTION

Most of us find that we have to attend formal functions at some point in our lives and they can be quite a strain to get through. The formality of these occasions means that we have to take care both to dress and behave correctly. We feel that we have to be on our best behaviour which in turn means that it is hard to relax.

Also, since these functions are rather few and far between, we often feel that we have to create and leave a good impression of ourselves. This can mean that we put an exaggerated value on the occasion and worry about getting things 'right' long before the actual event. This can cause us a lot of unnecessary stress.

Formal functions often involve other members of our family being present, as with weddings and christenings and so on, and when families get together on these sorts of occasions, stress and tension can develop for any number of reasons. When formal functions are connected with work, such as annual staff dinners, these too can make us tense and wary, depending on what might be at stake.

It is a pity that we so often regard these functions as a duty and dread them as they approach. Perhaps, by using these tips, the next one won't be quite such a stressful ordeal.

## WHAT TO DO

1 Your ability to relax at the function will be greatly helped if you learn and practise the following techniques in advance.
- Out-Breath Technique (*see page 30*).
- Deviation of Focus Technique (*see page 34*).
- Face (*see page 50*).
- Stomach (*see page 60*).
- Body Check (*see page 66*).

2 On both the evening before and the day of the actual function, execute the Deep Meditation Technique and the Total Relaxation with Mind-Clearing Technique (*see pages 68 and 46 respectively*). These two techniques will prepare you by relaxing you completely.

3 Check well in advance that you have everything you need to complete the outfit that you plan to wear. On the day of the function don't dress too

early, otherwise you will be worried that you might in some way damage or mark your clothes.

4 When you arrive, if you are alone, try to find someone that you know and go and speak to them. Alternatively, if you know no one, look around and see if you can find someone else who appears to be on their own. They will probably be as nervous as you and relieved to have someone to talk to and you can both comfort and commiserate with each other.

5 If you are having a conversation, try not to let your attention wander. It is easy on occasions such as these to feel small and insignificant, especially if you keep telling yourself what an important event it is.

Try, therefore, to detach yourself from your surroundings by concentrating on what is being said. You will be able to do this if you ask people about things that really interest you and listen closely to the replies.

6 If you get nervous or self-conscious and embarrassed, immediately put the Deviation of Focus Technique into action, really concentrating on things outside of yourself. You can couple this with the Out-Breath Technique if your breathing seems fast, and in a few moments you will be relaxed again.

7 Do a periodic Body Check, whether you are sitting or standing, to see if you are holding any muscles unnecessarily tightly. If you are, let them go.

8 Lastly, remember that although this is a formal function, it has been organized for people such as yourself to enjoy themselves or to celebrate or commemorate something. So try to divert your thoughts from yourself and instead remember why you are there.

## SEX – THE FIRST TIME

Many people assume that sex is automatically a happy and relaxed experience but the reverse is often the case. Sex can create great tension and anxiety. This is especially true at the start of a relationship, irrespective of our age or level of sexual experience. We worry and ask ourselves questions such as:

What will my partner expect of me?
Is my partner used to better and different sex?
Will the whole thing be a dismal failure?
Will I be good or experienced enough?
Supposing I don't or I can't respond?
What if I can't satisfy him or her?
If I really let go of my inhibitions, will I shock my partner?
Will he or she still like and be interested in me afterwards?
What if he or she doesn't like my body?
What if I don't like his or her body?

These and many other questions go round and round in our heads, creating extreme tension and stress.

Making love to someone is the closest that you can ever get physically to another human being. So close, in fact, that it is hard to hide our instantaneous reactions and feelings from that person. Exposing ourselves emotionally as well as physically in this way, when we are with somebody for the very first time, can be very scary.

This extreme closeness also means that physical love can be the most honest communication experienced between two people. It may be possible to pretend affection verbally, but when you touch somebody they will usually know the truth about what you feel for them.

Imagination, too, plays its part in causing a lot of fear and stress. It is very common, for example, to imagine that we know what the other person is thinking or feeling about us. Our minds can then get caught up in what I call the 'I think that he thinks that I think' syndrome. For example, a couple are making love for the first time. She thinks that he can't possibly like her body, so she tells herself that he is just making love to her for the sake of sex or because he

thinks it is expected of him. She decides that as he doesn't care, she will simply lie there and see it through without too much involvement, and so on. All this speculation causes a lot of confusion and misplaced hurt, and gets us nowhere. We are usually way off-beam anyway, so it is foolish to waste time and energy tormenting ourselves and worrying about what the other person might be thinking.

Try not to predict in advance what will happen when you make love. Your fear and anxiety will lead you to imagine all sorts of problems and complications that may never arise. Try not to think about the act of making love in a purely physical way, but think rather about the whole person. That means concentrating on what you like about them and their personalities. Why you like being with them and what you get out of the relationship. Sex may seem as if it concerns only particular parts of the body, but in fact you are making love to the whole person and that means their mind, body and emotions.

## The Importance of Relaxation in Sex

There is a sort of contradiction when making love, because in order to have good and satisfying sex one needs to be relaxed, yet at the same time able to get highly aroused and excited. You need the first in order to achieve the second, and so the ability to relax plays a large part in satisfying and fulfilling sex.

Love-making is usually best when both you and the atmosphere are calm, comfortable and relaxed. If you can reduce or eliminate as much tension, stress and anxiety as possible, you will be giving yourself the very best chance both to enjoy and to make a success of this very important part of your life.

## WHAT TO DO

**1** Don't have terribly high expectations the first time that you make love to somebody. Be realistic and tell yourself that couples need time to get to know each other's likes and dislikes and it is improbable, therefore, that the first time will be a spectacular success. Be prepared for this to be more of a 'getting to know each other' session.

**2** The first time you go to bed together you can relieve yourselves of much worry and pressure by making a joint decision that you don't intend, at all costs, to make love, but simply to lie and relax, and possibly to hold each other. This way it is very likely that, as you relax more, you will start to touch and caress each other and things will develop naturally.

**3** There is nothing guaranteed to bring about more stress than when sex is rushed. So really take your time and encourage your partner to do the same. This applies not only to intercourse itself, but the holding, touching, kissing and caressing that takes place before, during and after it.

**4** Tell your partner that you feel scared, wary, and so on if that is what you really feel. Being honest will allow him or her to reciprocate and bring you both closer.

**5** It is wonderful to stop and just concentrate on your own sensations for a while and not to feel that you have to do things to your partner all the time. You can take it in turns to do this for each other.

**6** Regular practice of the following techniques will not only help you to relax generally, but will also enable you to relax specific parts of your body during love-making if and when you feel yourself tensing up.

- Out-Breath Technique (*see page 30*).
- Stomach (*see page 60*).
- Buttocks (*see page 62*).
- Total Relaxation with Mind-Clearing Technique (*see page 46*).
- Deep Meditation Technique (*see page 68*).
- Body Check (*see page 66*).

**7** Should you start to feel nervous and stressed when making love, do a quick Body Check to see which muscles you might be holding unnecessarily tense, and let them go. Also, by performing the Out-Breath Technique a few times, you will quickly relax yourself again.

**8** Lastly, remember that satisfying sex for both you and your partner is all about enjoying sensations. The sensations can range in intensity from gentle arousal to exquisite climax, so allow yourself simply to feel these sensations and try not to worry or think of anything else during your love-making.

# OTHER COMMON STRESSFUL SITUATIONS

## TESTS AND EXAMS

Most of us will, at some time in our lives, have to take tests or exams, and we generally hate and dread them. We worry that we will not perform well and this, in itself, can create such stress that we indeed do not perform at our best when the time comes.

The fear associated with tests and exams is largely due to our anxiety about the consequences of failure. We worry that we will be disgraced and embarrassed if we fail, and not only for our own sake but often, more significantly, for the sake of those around us who expect us to do well. We don't want to let them down, and this can put an almost intolerable pressure on us.

Sometimes the tests or exams may be relatively unimportant but, in the majority of cases, they will carry with them the power to determine much about our lives. We are aware, therefore, that a lot depends on our success or failure, and our strong need to do well is such that we can create and live under the extreme stress and strain for weeks, if not months, before the time comes. We can often become so tense, nervous, anxious and worried that we don't sleep or eat properly, and the approaching test or exam can become an all-consuming obsession.

These dreaded events can also take on an inflated importance because we often see them as much more than they really are. We can, for example, begin to feel as though we are being tested personally as well as on the specific subject matter of the test or exam, and that our worth as people, whether we rate as successes or failures, is going to be judged on the results.

These thoughts and fears may not be on a conscious level but the effect that they can have on us is nevertheless very real and it adds dramatically to the stress and pressure that we are under.

In order to do one's best in any exam or test, we need to be able to let go of the inhibiting and sometimes mentally paralysing fear of failure. This we can do by learning and practising specific mental and physical techniques. One of the good things about most tests and exams is that we usually know about them in advance and this gives us adequate time to prepare thoroughly.

The following tips have been tried and tested with success. They will not, of course, perform miracles or teach you what you do not already know but they will help you to function at your best rather than at your worst.

## WHAT TO DO

**1** Practise the following techniques regularly until they are familiar to you. They will not only relax you during the run-up to your test or exam, but will greatly help you on the actual day itself.

- Out-Breath Technique (*see page 30*).
- Deviation of Focus Technique (*see page 34*).
- Sitting (*see page 36*).
- Neck (*see page 52*).
- Shoulders (*see page 56*).
- Arms, Hands and Fingers (*see page 58*).

- Total Relaxation with Mind-Clearing Technique (*see page 46*).
- Body Check (*see page 66*).

**2** Study and learn what you think you will need to know well in advance of your test or exam. I don't feel that it is a good idea to cram like mad at the last moment. Often all you will succeed in doing is throwing yourself into a panic, greatly increasing your anxiety and tension. It is better, if you can, to be a bit more philosophical at this stage, and to tell yourself that what you don't know now, you will probably not be able to learn in the time available anyway.

**3** The evening before your test or exam, execute the Total Relaxation with Mind-Clearing Technique. This can be particularly beneficial if it is done just before you retire or even when you are in bed, as it will help to promote a really good night's sleep and prepare you mentally and physically for the task ahead.

**4** On the day of your test or exam, before you leave home, try to have sufficient time to execute the following techniques slowly:

- Out-Breath Technique
- Shoulders
- Hands and Fingers
- Neck.

**5** Eat lightly on the day, and try to time your meals so that at least an hour will elapse between eating and the time of the test.

**6** Avoid wearing clothes that are tight around the waist or neck, as they will constrict your breathing.

**7** Aim to arrive at the place where the test or exam is going to be held with sufficient time to do everything that you need. Ideally, you should be able to put aside ten to fifteen minutes solely to relax yourself (*see* **8**) before the test begins. Add this time on to any extra time that you think you will need to do things such as finding the right room, depositing coats in cloakrooms, visiting the loo and attending to any other necessary details.

**8** Try to find a quiet corner where you won't be disturbed (often the loo can be as good a place as any), and repeat the same techniques listed under **4**. Try to have sufficient time left when you have completed these techniques so that you don't have to rush to the exam or test.

**9** When you enter the place where your test or exam is going to be held, immediately put the Deviation of Focus Technique into action. (You will need to have thought about this and done some homework before the day of the exam, following the instructions given with this Stress Cure on page 34).

**10** Assuming that you are sitting down for your test, before you begin adjust your position so that you are not holding any muscles unnecessarily tense, especially in your shoulders and arms.

**11** Be aware of your breathing and if you begin to feel tense immediately perform the Out-Breath Technique a few times.

**12** During the test or exam, concentrate on what you are being asked to do, rather than on yourself.

**13** If at any time you find yourself panicking, first of all do a quick Body Check to see if you are gripping any muscles that you don't need and, if you are, let them go.

Then combine the Out-Breath Technique with the Deviation of Focus Technique. All this will take no more than a few moments and it can restore you to a state of calm and relaxation. You can then continue. This emergency action can be repeated during the test or exam whenever necessary.

**Note:** *The Deviation of Focus Technique should not, of course, be done during a driving test or any other test that requires sustained, unbroken concentration.*

## GOING TO THE DENTIST

Many people have a dread of visiting the dentist even when it is merely for a check up but feel embarrassed to reveal this fear. It seems to them both silly and childish to be afraid since, as they tell themselves, 'everyone does it without making a fuss'.

For those of us who feel like this it may be some consolation to know that our fear of the dentist is both logical and justified. For one thing, as the treatment is being done in our mouths we are unable to see what is actually happening to us, and this in itself can be frightening. For another thing, we are robbed of our normal method of communication since our mouths are full of instruments and we are, therefore, unable to tell the dentist if we are in pain. Another of our very real fears is of the unknown. We often have no idea what is going to happen to us next, and this uncertainty can be very distressing.

It is not surprising, therefore, that visiting the dentist can put our minds, our bodies and our

emotions into an acute state of stress, and that many people put off visiting the dentist for as long as they can. Most of us, however, accept that we need to see the dentist on a regular basis if we are to have healthy teeth and gums, so our aim should be to remove, or, at least, to reduce as much stress as possible from these visits.

Dental treatment today is mainly painless. However, it is true to say that some of it can be uncomfortable, some can be extremely uncomfortable, and some can actually be painful although this is usually of short duration. If we were more prepared so that we knew in advance what we were likely to feel and how long the sensation would last, we would be less frightened and consequently more able to cope. Many dentists would be only too happy to co-operate by briefly explaining their procedures to their patients, but they are rarely asked. Patients tend to feel that they might appear 'weak' or 'foolish' if they ask questions about what is going to happen to them, or they are concerned that they are wasting the dentist's time, but this is not the case. He or she is there to serve you, and most dentists would feel that their time had been well spent if, at the end of it, they had a relaxed patient to treat rather than one squirming around in a high state of stress and tension.

Another common feeling when we visit the dentist is one of total vulnerability. Sitting or lying in the chair, our mouths wide open and full of dental paraphernalia, with the dentist on one side and the nurse on the other, it is no wonder that we feel trapped. It is then that the heart begins to race, the breath to quicken and the temperature to rise, as panic takes over. The frightening thing is that it can seem as though we have no control over these reactions. However, as you will see, it is possible to regain control and to calm yourself instantly and relax, even in these circumstances.

The following tips include specific relaxation techniques and advice. If you are nervous of going to the dentist, and each visit is a misery for you, then I would urge you to try them. They may not entirely eliminate your anxiety and fear, but they will certainly reduce them a little more each time you go.

## WHAT TO DO

1 Practise the following techniques regularly for a few days before your dental appointment.

- Out-Breath Technique (*see page 30*).
- Deviation of Focus Technique (*see page 34*).
- Total Relaxation Body Position (*see page 44*).
- Stomach (*see page 60*).
- Body Check (*see page 66*).

2 While you are in the waiting-room, sit well back in your seat with your legs uncrossed and your feet placed squarely on the floor. Put your bags and packages down and place your arms and hands where they can totally relax.

3 Concentrate on practising the Out-Breath Technique and the Deviation of Focus Technique. If you find it difficult to combine the two, then do them alternately.

4 When you are asked to go in to the surgery, try not to rush or get flustered. Think about collecting your things calmly, take a deep, smooth breath, then stand up and walk in.

5 When you go into the surgery, tell your dentist that you would like to have a word with him or her before the treatment or the check-up begins. Then tell the dentist of your fears. It is perfectly alright to say something like 'I am very nervous, so would you mind explaining to me what is going to happen before you begin each procedure and what I am likely to feel'. Also, since you won't be able to speak, ask the dentist to establish with you some kind of 'pain' signal that you can use to tell him or her if they are hurting you. It may be, for example, raising your right hand, or making a certain sound. Many dentists do, in fact, already do this, but you may need to clarify what the signal is for your own sense of security.

6 Most dental chairs are very comfortable these days, and some recline right back so that you are lying horizontally for your treatment. Take a few moments to settle yourself.

Then let your legs and feet fall open and relax, as you have been doing when practising the Total Relaxation Body Position. Place your arms and hands wherever you think they will be most comfortable, but if the chair has armrests, don't grip them. Allow your head to rest on the support provided. Now do a Body Check and let go of any muscles being held unnecessarily tense.

7 As treatment begins, concentrate completely on performing the Out-Breath Technique and, on each exhalation, feel as though you are sinking down and feeling really heavy and relaxed.

8 If you feel yourself tensing up at any time during the treatment, immediately do a further check, releasing any tensed muscles, then return once more to concentrating totally on the Out-Breath Technique.

**9** If you find your tension suddenly mounting uncontrollably, immediately perform the Deviation of Focus Technique, concentrating on it fully as previously instructed. The moment you feel calmer, return again to the Out-Breath Technique, feeling your body getting heavier each time you breathe out.

---

## VISITING OR CALLING THE DOCTOR

Visiting a doctor at a surgery or clinic, or calling one to your home in an emergency, can be a stressful and sometimes frustrating experience. To begin with, we may feel intimidated by the fact that the doctor is so knowledgeable whilst we, in contrast, know so little about the workings of our own bodies. This can make us feel foolish and inadequate.

Very often we fear that our complaint may be too trivial to justify bothering the doctor, and we consequently adopt an apologetic, almost guilty, attitude, feeling grateful that he or she is seeing us at all. We can become so inhibited and afraid that we don't ask the questions that we should about the complaint or the condition that is worrying us. We then end up frustrated and angry with ourselves for not having had the courage to be more assertive.

We hear and read a great deal about how overworked most doctors are, especially General Practitioners, and this can affect us to such a degree that we feel we have no right to take up more than a few short minutes of our doctor's time. This anxiety can sometimes mean that we accept whatever form of treatment is offered, without discussing it further to see if there might be a more agreeable alternative. We often think about these things later, however, and regret our haste.

Apart from guilt and diffidence, we may also experience embarrassment. After all, we often have to expose not only our bodies to our doctors, but also the most personal and intimate details about ourselves and our lives. This embarrassment can be felt even when we have known the doctor for some time. Many people suffer such acute stress and anxiety because of this that it can even prevent them from seeking medical help when they need it.

Whether to ask the doctor to call is a dilemma that many people face when they, their children, or other members of the household seem too ill to go to the surgery. They are afraid that the complaint might not be considered serious or urgent enough for a home visit. They worry because they don't want to 'inconvenience' the doctor, especially if it is during the night. They hesitate to 'bother' him or her unnecessarily and risk getting the reputation of being difficult patients. Yet another factor that influences and sometimes deters people from calling the doctor is fear and concern over what the doctor might think of their homes: is the house looking a mess? Doctors, of course, are used to visiting patients in all types of homes, and they usually have little time to notice the tidiness or otherwise of their surroundings. Remember that they are simply doing their job which is to take care of their patients.

Whatever the reason that deters people from calling out their doctors, the hesitation, deliberation and indecision create a great deal of stress – and do nothing to help the patient's condition.

When you need to see or call your doctor, there are several things that you can do that will help to eliminate your stress and anxiety. The following tips are divided into two sections. The first is designed to help when you go to visit your doctor, and the second for those occasions when your doctor visits you in your home.

## WHAT TO DO
### WHEN VISITING YOUR DOCTOR

1 Before your appointment, practise the following techniques:

- Sitting (*see page 36*).
- Body Check (*see page 66*).
- Out-Breath Technique (*see page 30*).

2 Make a list of your symptoms on a notepad beforehand and also all the questions that you want to ask your doctor. Take the notepad and a pen with you when you go.

3 Whilst in the waiting-room, sit back in your seat in the stress-free and relaxed position. If you begin to feel nervous or tense, practise the Out-Breath Technique a few times. Check through and think about the points on your list.

4 When you are called in to see the doctor, don't rush. Gather your things together, take a breath, stand up and walk in.

5 When you sit down, settle yourself as comfortably as you can in a relaxed position.

6 When your doctor asks what is wrong, say that there are several things you would like to ask, and that you have written them down so you won't forget them. The doctor now knows and is prepared for what is coming, and you can go calmly through your list.

7 Don't worry that you are taking up too much of the doctor's time. Let the doctor be the best judge of that. He or she knows approximately how long they can spend with each patient and they will certainly let you know in some way if they feel that your time is up. Generally speaking, a doctor will only rush a patient if they feel that the patient is wasting time by prolonging the visit unnecessarily. Most doctors appreciate patients who are organized enough to have prepared notes in advance, because it shows that they are taking an 'active' interest in their health. In my experience, the majority of doctors would far rather treat patients who ask questions than those who adopt an apathetic attitude, accepting whatever they are told.

8 If you feel nervous or tense, take a deep, smooth breath before you speak, and think about what you are saying, even if you are reading from your list.

9 Listen carefully to the doctor's responses and write down any comments and advice that you might want to remember later. Equally, you may want to jot down other notes or a follow-up question that may occur to you.

10 At any time during your visit, if you begin to get anxious, do a Body Check to see if you are holding any muscles unnecessarily tense.

If so, let them go, especially your shoulder and stomach muscles. Then execute the Out-Breath Technique a few times.

## WHAT TO DO
### WHEN YOUR DOCTOR IS VISITING YOU

1 If you feel tense or nervous whilst you are waiting for the doctor, whether you be the patient or not, try to stay as relaxed and as calm as you can by slowing your breathing down. You can do this by executing the Out-Breath Technique.

2 Think hard about the course of events that has led to you calling the doctor before he or she arrives. It is good to organize your thoughts in this way, because the doctor will immediately want information about what has happened as well as about any symptoms being experienced. If it is possible to write these things down, it is a good idea to do so in case you get a bit flustered and forget them when the doctor is with you.

3 When the doctor comes, try not to worry about what he or she is thinking. Concentrate entirely on the patient and what the patient is feeling. If it is you who is ill then give yourself permission to be a bit selfish and think about yourself.

4 It is fine for you to refer to your notes when describing the problem to the doctor. If you feel a bit awkward and tense, it is perfectly alright to say something like 'To make sure that I don't forget anything, I've written a few things down'. Then take a deep, smooth breath and speak as calmly and clearly

as you can, concentrating on what you are saying and on the doctor's response.

**5** Don't let the doctor leave until you have told him or her everything that seems relevant to the patient's condition and feel reasonably satisfied with the diagnosis, advice and treatment.

## HANDLING BUREAUCRACY

Dealing with bureaucracy is a necessity for most of us, but it is often a frustrating and extremely stressful experience. Frustrating, because it can seem that, in spite of our considerable efforts and sometimes long delays, we often don't appear to be getting anywhere. Many organisations that we have to deal with can seem faceless, cold and uncaring, but we are trapped because in order for our lives to run smoothly we have to communicate with them. For innumerable purposes, from finding out if we need planning permission to extend our homes, to securing a welfare payment to which we are entitled, there is no alternative to dealing with officialdom.

Bureaucracy and our reaction to it can create a lot of stress. A typical example might go as follows.

We telephone a particular organisation in order to query a bill. We explain our query calmly and in great detail, only to be told that somebody else deals with it. We are then transferred and have to explain it all again. They, of course, may well transfer us on yet again, by which time we hate the person on the other end of the phone, want nothing more to do with the whole affair and slam the phone down, feeling hot, flustered and furious. The trouble with this reaction, understandable though it is, is that it merely postpones the problem and gets us into a state of stress.

We need to know how best to handle bureaucracy so that we get what we want without ending up tense, nervous and fraught.

## WHAT TO DO

**1** Remember that although you are dealing with an organisation, it is run by individual human beings much like yourself. It may, therefore, help greatly if you can find out the name of the person that you are dealing with at the outset and then address him or her by it. This can often improve your relationship with the person concerned, making them feel more disposed towards you.

**2** Have as much information to hand as possible when you are dealing with any bureaucratic organisation. Likewise, any relevant documents, papers, bills and so on.

**3** List all your queries or problems clearly on a piece of paper before making contact.

**4** Whether you make contact by telephone or in person, the calmer you can remain the better. Prepare for this by practising the Out-Breath Technique (*see page 30*) and the Body Check (*see page 66*).

**5** Much time is spent waiting around when dealing with bureaucracy, and often this can mean sitting in a queue, sometimes for hours, and getting more and more steamed up as time goes by. You can counteract this in two ways.

Firstly, if there is nothing that you can do about it, you have to accept the fact that you must wait, but this needn't turn into a stressful experience. If you practise the technique for Sitting in advance (*see page 36*), you can do this while you wait so that your body becomes and stays relaxed.

Secondly, plan in advance to use the waiting time constructively, by taking something with you to do. Writing overdue letters, for example, or making notes about things that you are planning or have to do in the future. Alternatively, of course, you can take a good book. The important thing is to go prepared. It may surprise you to find how quickly time flies by when you are absorbed in something.

**6** You will achieve the best results for yourself if you are neither aggressive nor passive. You need to be as clear as you can be about your requirements and assertive in your attitude, so that you communicate well. You will find the tips in the section *How to be more Assertive* (*see below*) a great help in this respect.

**7** Before you speak, always take a deep, smooth breath, and talk calmly and clearly, thinking about your words and their meaning as you say them. Try not to interrupt the other person if possible, and listen carefully to their reply. If you are not satisfied or you don't understand, say so pleasantly, something along the lines of 'It's probably my fault, but I seem to be in a bit of confusion. Could you please help me to sort it out?'. Most people working in bureaucratic organisations are reasonable, and if you show them consideration they are likely to reciprocate.

**8** During your exchange, if you begin to feel tense or anxious, do a Body Check and release any muscles that are being gripped unnecessarily. Then perform the Out-Breath Technique a few times. You will quickly restore yourself to a calm, relaxed state.

**9** Lastly, remember that official organisations are there to serve you as a member of the public. You are, therefore, perfectly entitled to any time and attention that either you or your problems require.

---

# HELPING YOURSELF

## HOW TO BE MORE ASSERTIVE

Let's first of all establish if you need to be more assertive. Answer the following questions truthfully.

Do you find yourself often saying 'Yes' when you really mean 'No'?

Do you get anxious and worried when you have to refuse somebody something?

Do you find it difficult to voice your true opinion or to get your point across?

Do you find it difficult to complain, especially in public?

Do you accept excuses from others even when you feel that you have been 'fobbed off'?

Do you have difficulty in expressing verbally love and affection to those whom you care about?

Do you have difficulty in expressing disapproval?

Do you accept second-rate service rather than 'make a fuss'?

Do you avoid arguments at all costs, even when you feel you are right?

Do you 'bottle things up' rather than lose your temper?

Do you often feel manipulated by others?

If you answer *YES* to some of these and other similar questions, then it is likely that you are creating for yourself a lot of unnecessary stress, strain and anxiety. Learning to be more assertive can not only eliminate this stress and tension from your life, but also greatly improve your self-esteem and confidence, making life much more rewarding and satisfying.

## What do We Actually Mean by 'Assertiveness'?

Many people think, wrongly, that in order to be assertive one has to be aggressive, but that isn't so. Being assertive is simply being able to communicate your thoughts, feelings, desires and requirements clearly and effectively to others, in neither a passive nor an aggressive way.

It is not surprising that in the past women have had more difficulty than men in being assertive. Assertiveness has been confused with and linked to aggression which was always considered a very masculine characteristic. Women, not wanting to be thought of as masculine, tried not to behave in what was regarded as an 'inappropriate', 'unattractive' and certainly 'unfeminine' way. Fortunately many women now appreciate that there is nothing unfeminine in being assertive and are beginning to have the confidence to express themselves in a clear, honest and straightforward way. This is, after all, what being assertive means, whether you are male or female.

Assertiveness also means not being too worried and preoccupied that your behaviour doesn't fit in with other people's images and ideas of how you 'ought' to be. After all, if that is a problem for them, then it is just that, 'their problem'. You have no need to accept responsibility for it. Let them deal with it as best they can.

We are brought up to be polite to those around us and we quickly get used to reacting in, as we see it, the most inoffensive way possible. This means that in order to maintain the *status quo* we often have to pretend and lie to others to avoid conflict and confrontation. This, far from leading to a satisfactory life, can cost

us much in terms of our happiness, contentment and fulfilment.

Although reacting 'honestly' can be a frightening prospect for some people if they are not used to doing it, learning to be more assertive can certainly change lives for the better. These tips are designed to help you begin that process of transformation.

## WHAT TO DO

**1** Being able to relax physically and to breathe properly are the most relevant and valuable assets that you can have in learning to become more assertive. Usually the body tenses and breathing becomes restricted at the slightest sign of anxiety, nervousness or stress and your ability to communicate calmly and clearly will be affected. You therefore need to be able to 'untense' yourself immediately. To help you with this, begin to practise the following techniques on a regular basis.

- Out-Breath Technique (*see page 30*).
- Face (*see page 50*).
- Shoulders (*see page 56*).
- Stomach (*see page 60*).
- Body Check (*see page 66*).
- Total Relaxation with Mind-Clearing Technique (*see page 46*).

**2** The golden rule when nervous is, firstly, to use the Out-Breath Technique a few times, which will calm you down. Then, *always* take a deep, smooth breath and try to talk calmly and clearly, thinking hard about what you are saying.

**3** When we receive a request or an invitation, we often feel that we need to reply instantly. Consequently we immediately put ourselves under considerable and quite unnecessary strain. There is nothing wrong with delaying your answer and saying something like 'I'd like to think about that' or 'Can I let you know later?' or other similar phrases. This frees you from pressure and gives you the time to think coolly about what you really want to do. Unless you know for sure that you want to accept something, it is always safest to take a deep, smooth breath and tell the other person calmly that you will let them know.

**4** During a conversation, debate or discussion, if you are finding it difficult for some reason to get your point across, it will often help if you actually admit what you feel. For example, you can say something like 'I feel really bad about saying this to you, but I disagree'. Then say why and put your point forward calmly and clearly. Or, you could say 'I find this really embarrassing, but I just don't like this food, place, person or whatever'. Without being rude, it is usually possible to let the person that you are communicating with know exactly what you think.

**5** It will be a great help to you if you can begin to practise saying the word '*No*' just on its own. Start off by using it when you are dealing with relatively insignificant things such as when you go shopping or when you are making 'small talk' with friends, neighbours or colleagues. You may be surprised at how good and strong using that word on its own can make you feel. When your confidence has grown a bit, start to use it when appropriate for the more important issues in your life.

**6** No matter what the situation, should you begin to feel nervous, tense or stressed, immediately begin the Out-Breath Technique and execute it slowly, as instructed, a few times. You will quickly find yourself restored to a calm, relaxed state. Do this as often as necessary.

**7** Lastly, don't expect to become completely assertive in every possible way overnight. It takes time for your confidence to build, especially if you have spent a large part of your life giving way to others. However, using these tips, you will find yourself growing steadily stronger and, therefore, able to handle the situations in your life in an increasingly effective way.

## HOW TO BE LESS SELF-CONSCIOUS

How we appear to others can concern us to such a degree that it becomes a source of great anxiety, tension, embarrassment and stress.

Most of us feel self-conscious at certain times in our lives and it can be an extremely unpleasant and unsettling process.

As small children, we don't know what it is to be self-conscious. We just behave in a natural and uninhibited way. Quite early, however, we are taught that it's rude to stare, bad manners to talk with our mouths full and that we must say 'please' and 'thank you' instead of grabbing what we want. As we grow up, self-consciousness increases sharply. By the time we are teenagers we start to compare ourselves constantly to others, usually to our own detriment. We become dissatisfied with ourselves, spending hours in front of a mirror, criticising the length of our legs or the colour of our hair. Whatever we've been born with is somehow *wrong* – we want to be different from the way we are.

With some people, this process takes its course and they emerge several years later as adults having accepted, in the main, that they are what they are and that they will have to learn to live with their imperfections and faults. Other people find that strong feelings of embarrassment and self-consciousness stay with them well into adulthood or return periodically, causing them anxiety and pain. There is a third group of people who, retaining the extreme self-consciousness of adolescence, suffer to such an extent that how they look, sound or come across to other people becomes an obsession that dominates their existence. Such can be their distress that they actually avoid contact where possible, severely restricting their personal, social and business lives.

Whichever category you fit into, if you suffer from self-consciousness you are causing yourself unnecessary anguish and stress. It is possible, however, to learn how to liberate yourself from these feelings, transforming your life as a result, and the following tips have been designed to help you do just that.

## WHAT TO DO

**1** When we become self-conscious, we stiffen up physically and we mentally become 'fixed' on ourselves. We need, therefore, to prepare so that we can instantly 'let go' to order when the situation demands it. By practising the following techniques you will not only be doing this, but also relaxing yourself generally.

- Out-Breath Technique (*see page 30*).
- Deviation of Focus Technique (*see page 34*).
- Body Check (*see page 66*).
- Face (*see page 50*).
- Shoulders (*see page 56*).
- Arms, Hands and Fingers (*see page 58*).
- Legs and Feet (*see page 64*).
- Stomach (*see page 60*).
- Buttocks (*see page 62*).
- Total Relaxation with Mind-Clearing Technique (*see page 46*).

You do not necessarily have to practise all the above in one go. However, the first three techniques will be of crucial importance to you when feeling self-conscious and should, therefore, be regarded as a priority and practised regularly until they become familiar. The other techniques are also very valuable, but can be practised on a slightly less regular basis.

**Note:** *No matter where you are, or what you are doing, the moment you feel self-conscious one or all three of the following tips should be followed and then repeated as often as necessary.*

**2** Perform the Deviation of Focus Technique, concentrating totally on things outside yourself, as instructed.

**3** Do a really thorough Body Check. Systematically go through your body releasing any muscles that you are gripping unnecessarily, paying particular attention to your stomach, shoulders and face.

**4** Do the Out-Breath Technique several times, until you feel that you are calmer and more relaxed.

**Note:** *In time, and with practice, it may be possible for you to perform all three of the above techniques simultaneously.*

**5** We often feel self-conscious when we think that people are either observing us or that they are critical of us or our behaviour. The plain truth is that the majority of people are so absorbed in themselves and their own lives that they just don't have the time and energy to devote to such thoughts about other people. It would be easy, for example, to torment yourself by thinking that, when somebody glances your way, they are in some way judging you. In reality, they will probably hardly have noticed you. Remember this and apply it in other situations in your life when you are feeling self-conscious.

**6** If you can take an interest in or get involved with almost anything or anyone outside your own thoughts and feelings, it will bring about immediate release and relief when you are feeling self-conscious. This works even if your interest or involvement only lasts for a few short moments.

**7** At the beginning, you may find that you have to repeat some of the above tips, possibly even several times. This depends largely on how much self-consciousness affects your life. However, as you use the techniques, you will gradually become less and less dependent on them as your self-consciousness diminishes.

**Note:** See also *Self-Consciousness and Self-Awareness (page 15).*

# THE WEEKENDER –
# THE TOTAL STRESS CURE WEEKEND

When we think of taking a holiday, we think of packing a suitcase and rushing off somewhere. Holidays of this type, however, can often be quite stressful and, in any case, most of us aren't able to leave our homes, jobs and so on at a moment's notice. If you are feeling really stressed and want to do something about it now, you can have a wonderfully quick and relaxing break in your own home if you know how to go about it.

'The Weekender', as the name implies, is just a weekend break, taken in your own home. By following the total relaxation and stress elimination plan given below, you can successfully relieve yourself in one short weekend of your stress, anxiety and tension, but you must follow the instructions carefully.

## WHAT TO DO

**1** Cancel every appointment and long-standing arrangement that you may have for your chosen weekend, and tell everyone that you are going to be unavailable.

**2** Stock up with enough food and drink to see you through the weekend, bearing in mind that you are going to be on a relatively light diet.

**3** Hide all watches and clocks by putting them in drawers or cupboards well out of your sight.

**4** The telephone is going to be completely out of bounds during this weekend, so un-plug it or turn it off, if possible. Otherwise, try to muffle the sound of it as much as you can by putting pillows, blankets, towels, or anything else that you can think of over it, so that you won't hear it when it rings. Alternatively, if you are convinced that you can be disciplined enough *not* to answer the telephone if it rings, just simply leave it as it is.

**5** Your 'Weekender' starts officially on Friday evening. From then on, resolve not to watch television or listen to the radio. Unplug them if that helps your resolve.

**6** Eat a very light supper and aim to be in bed by 10 p.m. at the latest. Read something undemanding and soothing and, if you like, you can listen to some gentle music, but stay in bed.

**7** Whilst lying in bed, before you go to sleep, practise the Out-Breath Technique (*see page 30*), increasing the number of repetitions to twenty, breathing out really slowly as directed. Follow with the Total Relaxation with Mind-Clearing Technique (*see page 46*). This will help you to drift into a relaxed sleep.

**8** Whatever time you wake up on Saturday morning, stay put. Your bed is going to be your base for the entire weekend and you are not going to get dressed, bathed, shaved or bother with any other of your normal daily routine. It is fine, however, to get yourself a drink and perhaps some light breakfast, but take it back to bed.

**9** Spend your time daydreaming, wafting off to sleep now and again if it happens, or listening to soft music with your eyes closed.

**10** As the day progresses, don't make yourself elaborate meals. It is better to have perhaps some fruit, cheese and biscuits on a tray in your bedroom, so that you can just pick at the food from time to time when you are hungry. It is also a good idea to have handy a large jug of fruit juice or water.

**11** Twice during the day on Saturday, at no specific times, get out of bed and slowly execute the Deep Meditation Technique (*see page 68*), returning to bed again afterwards. Try to allow a few hours between the repetitions of this technique, but judge it as best you can without actually looking at the time.

**12** Continue to loll around in bed for the rest of Saturday. Take food and drink when and if you need it, but don't be tempted to check the time. The fading light will tell you when evening comes.

**13** When you begin to feel tired, perform the Out-Breath Technique twenty times, followed by the Total Relaxation with Mind-Clearing Technique.

**14** When you wake on Sunday, proceed exactly as for Saturday, but do the Deep Meditation Technique *three* times at intervals during the day.

**15** After dusk has fallen and not before, retrieve your clocks and watches from their hiding places and organize any alarms you may need for Monday morning.

**16** Read or listen to some gentle music once more if you like, and when you begin to feel a little sleepy, no matter what time it is, put the lights out. Perform the Out-Breath Technique twenty times followed by the Total Relaxation with Mind-Clearing Technique.

If you have followed the instructions, Monday morning should find you relaxed, refreshed and well rested.

Repeat the 'Weekender' as often as you like. If you should feel your stress returning during the subsequent days, weeks or months, I suggest that you use some of the above tips to reduce or remove that stress. For example, at home in the evening, practise the Deep Meditation Technique, then eat lightly and go to bed early. Once in bed, perform the Out-Breath Technique twenty times, followed by the Total Relaxation with Mind-Clearing Technique.

## ADDITIONAL TIPS TO CUT OUT STRESS

The following three tips, although seemingly trivial, can have a remarkable effect in both stress reduction and elimination. There is no technique to learn and you can, with a little bit of thought, immediately implement them into your life. I really urge you to try them and see for yourself how these simple behavioural modifications can help.

## Touching

*Touch someone and show you care.*
The importance of touching and of making physical contact with other people, in both reducing and eliminating stress, cannot be over-emphasized. It really can work wonders and bring tremendous relief of tension. I am not, of course, recommending that you go around touching *everybody*, but try to increase the number of times that you touch, hold and, if appropriate, cuddle the people closest to you and that you care about. Stroking a pet can have a similarly relaxing effect.

## Smiling

*If you are stressed, try to make a point of smiling at someone at least once every day.*
You may be really surprised at how good it can feel if you look right at somebody and give them a broad and genuine smile. The person can be a total stranger or someone that you know quite well, but your aim should be to make *them*, rather than *you*, feel good. In actual fact, it will make you feel very good too because it forces you to concentrate momentarily on something and someone outside yourself. This has a wonderfully relaxing and therapeutic effect. Try it.

## Say How You 'Really' Feel

*Tell at least one person each day how you really feel.*
When asked how we are, we automatically answer 'fine', but often it isn't the truth. It will both comfort you and disperse your stress if you know that even one other person in the world knows how you feel. This doesn't necessarily have to be someone you know well, it could be the local shopkeeper or the postman, and it doesn't mean that you have to go into lengthy explanations about your particular problems. It just means that, when asked

how you are, you can say something like 'Actually, today I feel really worried, sad, angry, depressed', and so on. By making this type of remark, you are not asking the other person for help necessarily, but just verbalizing your feelings can have a strangely liberating effect, freeing you from a lot of stress.

# STRESS CURE C
## Stress-Related Medical and Psychological Problems

At one time, it was thought that stress affected us in a purely psychological way. We now know, however, that stress can also have an extremely dramatic effect on the body itself, causing or exacerbating all kinds of conditions and complaints. These can range from trivial to severe and can cause mild irritation to acute pain.

Many of the conditions covered in this section can be so painful, uncomfortable, or inconvenient that life becomes an absolute misery. Other conditions can cause extreme worry, anxiety, nervousness and depression.

With some conditions, it is not always absolutely clear whether stress has caused the condition or the condition has caused the stress. However, the removal or reduction of the stress can often be one of the key elements in bringing about improvement or even total recovery.

The tips, suggestions and advice in this section are designed to help relieve and sometimes to prevent the various conditions and complaints listed here. By following them, you may be able to ease or completely eliminate your problem from your life.

**Note:** *Although the conditions in this section are commonly caused by or greatly contributed to by stress, it is important to point out that your condition may be entirely due to medical causes and have nothing whatever to do with stress. If you are in any doubt, I would strongly recommend that you see your doctor so that you are able to clarify the situation and obtain the appropriate treatment.*

## ALLERGIES

Allergies can show themselves in many ways and can have very many causes. They can, for example, be caused by an intolerance of or a reaction to certain foods, plants, chemicals, fabrics, environments, and a whole host of other things. Some even remain a mystery in terms of their origin.

Allergies can be extremely disturbing and debilitating to the sufferer and can cause such things as itching, skin rashes, repeated sneezing, asthma, nausea, vomiting, headache, migraine, stomach upsets, fever and many, many other conditions.

Much stress can be experienced by people suffering from allergies, not least because they are having to put up with repeated physical discomfort. Reducing this stress and being able to relax more can go a long way towards the toleration, reduction or even total alleviation of the allergy.

If you suffer from an allergy, you might like to try these tips.

## WHAT TO DO

In order to remove stress and be generally more relaxed, practise the following techniques on a regular basis.
- Out-Breath Technique (*see page 30*).
- Total Relaxation with Mind-Clearing Technique (*see page 46*).
- Deep Meditation (*see page 68*).

## ASTHMA

Asthma is a condition that can be greatly affected by stress, with attacks sometimes being precipitated or made much worse by it. Asthma sufferers can, therefore, often greatly help themselves by removing or reducing their stress.

Learning how to relax generally will be very helpful, and also learning how to relax and slow the breathing down when it feels as though an attack is imminent. This can lessen the severity of the attack and sometimes even stop it altogether.

## WHAT TO DO

I Learn and practise the following techniques on a regular basis.

- Out-Breath Technique (*see page 30*).
- Natural Tranquillizing Technique (*see page 32*).
- Shoulders (*see page 56*).
- Total Relaxation with Mind-Clearing Technique (*see page 46*).

2 When you feel your breathing quickening up and sense that an attack may be imminent, execute the Out-Breath Technique, doing it very slowly as instructed. Continue for several minutes or until you feel your breathing calming down.

3 Often during an asthmatic attack the shoulder muscles will automatically tense up and tighten. Therefore, once your breathing has become more normal and regular, execute the Shoulders Technique, exactly in the way that you have been practising it.

## BACK PAIN

Tension and stress can cause us to grip certain of our back and shoulder muscles without realizing it. This can lead to back pain, which in turn increases our stress, and so it goes on.

It will therefore be a great help to you, if you are a back pain sufferer, to both eliminate the stress and the muscle tension when it occurs, and that is what these tips are designed to do.

## WHAT TO DO

I Practise the following techniques on a regular basis. They will relax you generally and prepare you so that you can relieve your back pain.

- Total Relaxation with Mind-Clearing Technique (*see page 46*).
- Top of the Back (*see page 54*).
- Shoulders (*see page 56*).
- Body Check (*see page 66*).

2 If and when your back starts to hurt, do a Body Check and if you are holding any muscles unnecessarily tense, let them go.

**3** If, after executing the above technique, your back still feels painful or tense, perform the Top of the Back Technique and the Shoulders Technique, both of which are planned to provide instant relaxation.

**4** Next, lie down with your back flat on the floor and execute the Total Relaxation with Mind-Clearing Technique, remaining in the position afterwards for as long as your time allows.

**5** Backache can have many causes, but here are some simple do's and don'ts.

## DO'S

● Do sleep on a hard bed, flat on your back. See *Sleeping (page 43)*.

● Do keep your weight down to that recommended for your height and build.

● Do try to do some gentle form of exercise such as yoga, to keep your back flexible and strong.

## DON'TS

● Don't bend over to lift heavy objects with a rounded back. Try to keep your back straight and bend well at the knees.

● Don't suddenly decide to do a lot of physical work such as gardening, where you are crouching over for prolonged periods, especially when you haven't done this for some time. It is best to strengthen your back muscles by beginning with only a few minutes' work, and then gradually building up.

● Don't suddenly twist your body around or reach high up to get something, even when in a hurry.

● Don't carry excessively heavy objects if you can possibly avoid it. If you must carry heavy things, try to distribute the weight evenly by splitting the load and carrying it in both hands.

● Don't sleep on a soft bed or with more than one pillow.

---

## CONSTIPATION

Constipation can be an extremely debilitating condition and can affect our lives in many ways. It can lead to irritability, tiredness, depression, lack of appetite and nausea, among other things.

Stress plays a particularly large part in contributing to this condition, because being aware that we are constipated makes us anxious and tense, making the constipation very much worse. This is the case whether we suffer from it chronically or just from time to time. The following tips may help.

## WHAT TO DO

**1** If you suffer from constipation, it is important to be able to relax generally, and also to relax specific and especially relevant muscle groups. In order to do this, practise the following techniques regularly:

● Out-Breath Technique (*see page 30*).
● Natural Tranquillizing Technique (*see page 32*).
● Total Relaxation with Mind-Clearing Technique (*see page 46*).
● Stomach (*see page 60*).

**2** Check your diet to make sure that you are eating enough roughage and, if not, adjust it accordingly.

**3** Try to eat some fresh fruit every day.

**4** Try to drink at least a litre of water each day.

**5** Some people find it helps to start the day with a drink of hot boiled water with a squeeze of lemon juice and honey.

**6** Go for a brisk twenty-minute walk at least once a day, following the breathing instructions given under *Walking (see page 38)*.

7 Don't eat a big meal just before going to bed. Instead, try to eat at least three hours before retiring.

8 Allow as much time as you can for 'relaxing' when you go to the loo. Nothing increases constipation more than the nervousness and tension created by having to rush. It is also a good idea to take some reading matter in with you to take your mind off your problem.

9 Whilst on the loo, practise the Out-Breath Technique and also the Stomach Technique, to help you to relax.

# DYSMENORRHOEA (PERIOD PAIN)

The degree of period pain suffered by many women can range from mild to so severe that the sufferer literally has to take to her bed.

There are many medical causes of dysmenorrhoea, but it is also thought that stress can be a contributory factor. It will, therefore, help to ease the condition if you can reduce or eliminate as much stress and tension as possible.

## WHAT TO DO

1 If you suffer from period pain, practise the following techniques regularly. They will not only relax you generally but will be of great help to you when you are actually suffering from the condition.
- Out-Breath Technique (see page 30).
- Natural Tranquillizing Technique (see page 32).
- Lying (see page 42).
- Total Relaxation with Mind-Clearing Technique (see page 46).
- Body Check (see page 66).

2 When you become aware of pain, either in the abdominal area or in the lower back, if it is possible lie flat on your back as in the Total Relaxation position. Execute the Out-Breath Technique a few times and then the Total Relaxation with Mind-Clearing Technique. If it is more comfortable, it is fine to execute these techniques lying on your back, but with your knees bent, legs apart, and the soles of your feet flat on the floor.

3 Heat, applied in the form of a hot water bottle, can greatly soothe and relieve the pain whether it is in the abdominal area or the lower back.

4 If you are not able to lie down, try sitting comfortably and then practise the Natural Tranquillizing Technique, really concentrating as instructed.

5 If you are in a situation where you simply cannot take time out to either sit or lie and relax for a while, do a Body Check to see if you are holding any muscles tense. If you are, then let them go, paying particular attention to your stomach muscles. The Out-Breath Technique will also help you to relax no matter what situation you are in.

6 When you are likely to suffer from period pain, try to remember not to wear clothes that are particularly tight around the waist.

7 Try to avoid as much tension and pressure as you can during the painful days and try not to get embroiled in situations that will add to your stress. Don't demand too much of yourself and have as much rest and relaxation as you can.

8 Eating heavily can sometimes exacerbate this condition, so try to eat a light diet around this time of the month.

9 There is a particular yoga movement that is especially beneficial in reducing or eliminating period pain, and you may care to try it.

**1.** Get on hands and knees, with the knees and feet open a few inches. Arch your back slowly, pushing the pelvis forward and letting your head relax forward too. Hold the position still for a slow count to five.

**2.** Slowly reverse the position, hollowing your back out, pushing your bottom up and raising your head as much as you can. Hold that position still for a count of five and repeat the entire up and down movement a further five times.

## EYESTRAIN

Eyestrain can be due to many factors and can be uncomfortable and distressing. If you turn to *Eyes* (*see page 48*), you will find advice on how to relax your eyes instantly and other tips on how to deal with this condition.

## FATIGUE

We all feel tired and worn out at times, but there are periods in our lives, particularly when we are under stress, when our fatigue is excessive and it starts to concern us.

We feel lethargic and tired to the point that we could easily lounge around all day, and our enthusiasm for doing the things that we usually enjoy is somehow missing. Lethargy leads to more lethargy, which in turn can lead to depression and anxiety. We need, therefore, to see if we can energize and revitalize ourselves.

### WHAT TO DO

**1** The first essential in counteracting fatigue is to make sure that you are getting good quality rest when you go to sleep at night. That means mentally as well as physically. Read and follow the advice given in *Sleeping* (*see page 43*).

**2** The following breathing procedure can have a revitalizing and refreshing effect, and should be practised three times a day. Try to do it near an open window so that you are taking in fresh air and oxygen.

● Stand square, legs and feet about a foot and a half apart, arms and hands relaxed at your sides.

● Take a really strong breath in through the nose for four counts.

● Exhale by blowing the breath out strongly through the mouth for four counts.

Repeat both the inhalation and exhalation a total of ten times.

**3** Take a brisk twenty-minute walk at least twice a day, following the instructions given under *Walking* (*see page 38*) and taking particular care to breathe as directed.

**4** Eat relatively lightly but make sure that you are getting all the essential vitamins and minerals.

**5** We sometimes get excessively fatigued at moments in our lives when we have to make important decisions. The fatigue can be a kind of psychological escape or withdrawal. It is, therefore, sometimes beneficial to let yourself temporarily off the hook by making a decision *not* to make any decisions for the moment. Removing the pressure from yourself in this way can often be the turning point.

**6** When we are very fatigued and concerned about it, we can wrongly feel ashamed and lazy, and this can lead to great stress. It is a good idea, therefore, to try to communicate honestly with those around you about how you feel. Being able to verbalize your thoughts and feelings like this can go a long way towards rapid recovery.

**7** Sometimes, when under great stress, your entire organism simply decides that it has had enough and that it needs to 'over-ride' your wishes and take time out in which to gently recuperate. When the body and the mind are sufficiently rested, your fatigue will automatically disappear, but it may have to happen in its own time. Remember this, go along with it and don't despair because you will come out of it.

---

# FLATULENCE

Flatulence or wind is a perfectly normal and biological necessity. Our bodies produce between one and two litres of gas each day, and this inevitably has to pass out of our bodies in one way or another.

Wind can not only be physically painful, but also psychologically distressing because in our society so much embarrassment surrounds it. The results of this can be worry, anxiety and stress. The problem is that many of us have strong and very deep-seated guilt feelings about this particular biological function, which may have had their origins in infancy. We learned as children that passing wind was a bad or even a dirty thing to do, and it was consequently never talked about.

We may be fully-fledged adults now, but our feelings of shame haven't lessened, only deepened. We worry, fret and tense up at the 'horrendous' social consequences of breaking wind in public. The stress that this causes, ironically, can make the problem much worse.

Some people are affected to such an extent that they develop a severe complex, which in turn can seriously affect their lives and relationships.

Stress, of course, is not the only contributory factor where flatulence is concerned. There are also many things that we do unconsciously that can greatly add to the problem. If you suffer from excessive wind, I suggest that you try some of the following tips.

## WHAT TO DO

**1** Practise these techniques until they are familiar because they may be valuable in dealing with your problem.

● Out-Breath Technique (*see page 30*).
● Stomach (*see page 60*).
● Body Check (*see page 66*).

**2** Certain foods are commonly known to produce an excessive amount of gas. For example, beans, Brussels sprouts, cabbage, root vegetables and nuts.

Foods, however, affect different people in very different ways, and you must discover for yourself by trial and error which foods adversely affect you, then try either to avoid or reduce your intake of them. When you do eat these foods, masticate well before swallowing.

**3** People who suffer from excessive flatulence often swallow a lot of air when they eat. To counteract this, eat slowly, chewing each mouthful throughly before swallowing.

**4** When eating, pause between mouthfuls, put your knife and fork down and sit back in your seat. Perform the Out-Breath Technique a few times to help you to relax for a few moments before you return to your food.

**5** If you like to drink at mealtimes, don't gulp the drink down and also try to avoid carbonated drinks or colas.

**6** Chewing gum can cause a lot of wind, as can smoking, so try to cut down or eliminate these habits altogether if you can.

**7** When we are in conversation and feel stressed or nervous, we often gulp air as we speak instead of breathing properly. Try to be conscious, therefore, of your breathing, and always make a point of taking a deep, smooth breath before you begin to talk.

**8** Another unconscious reaction when we are nervous is to suck our stomach muscles in. This too can create additional wind as it disturbs the digestive process. Do periodic checks to see if you are gripping these muscles and, if you are, let them go.

**9** The more generally relaxed you are the more this problem will diminish. Therefore, no matter what situation you are in, if you begin to tense up or become nervous do a Body Check to see if you are holding any muscles unnecessarily tightly and let them go.

**10** Lastly, remember that everyone has the same biological functions as you. Take comfort, therefore, from the fact that no matter who you are with, they too will suffer and experience exactly the same uncomfortable and embarrassing feelings about wind as you do.

---

## HEADACHE

Headaches are among the most common conditions suffered as a result of tension and stress, and although this complaint is often regarded as very trivial, it can be an extremely unpleasant, painful and debilitating experience, especially when the headaches frequently recur.

There is often little sympathy for headache sufferers because many people regard headaches as a minor complaint. They feel that in order to succumb to it one must be a bit 'feeble' or 'pathetic'. The headache is also looked upon as a classic, quick and convenient excuse when somebody wants to opt out.

A headache should, however, be treated seriously for it is an undeniable physiological reaction and signifies that something is wrong.

Whether you suffer frequently or just now and again, it is a good idea to examine the circumstances surrounding your headaches to see if you can discover what might be the physical, mental or emotional trigger for them. You can then try to avoid these in the future. Headaches can be caused by many factors, some of which are listed below.

Relaxation plays a very large part in both the prevention and the cure of headaches, so it is a good idea to learn how to relax generally in one's life as well as specifically when the headaches come. To this end, the regular practice of certain of the techniques, as recommended, will help greatly. You will also find further tips on prevention which you might find useful.

## WHAT TO DO

**1** Practise the following techniques regularly. Some will be particularly valuable when trying to eliminate a headache when it occurs.

- Natural Tranquillizing Technique (*see page 32*).
- Out-Breath Technique (*see page 30*).
- Lying Down (*see page 42*).
- Total Relaxation with Mind-Clearing Technique (*see page 46*).
- Eyes (*see page 48*).
- Neck (*see page 52*).
- Shoulders (*see page 56*).
- Body Check (*see page 66*).

**2** These are some common reasons and situations that can be the causes of headaches. See if they ring a bell with you and, if they do, avoid them if at all possible.

Excessively hot or noisy places.
Smoke-filled areas.
Heated arguments.
Missing meals.
Over-eating.
Constipation.
Excessively bright lighting.
Dull or dim lighting.
Working for long periods at a *VDU* screen.
Watching television for long periods of time.
Reading or studying for long periods.
Not getting enough fresh air.
Not eating a balanced diet.
Not sleeping well.

**3** Since worry, anxiety and tension are responsible for many headaches, think about what is currently going on in your life and what might be causing such stress. Then see if you can in any way improve things.

**4** The next time that you get a headache, find somewhere quiet and private and practise the Natural Tranquillising Technique, increasing the number of repetitions to ten.

**5** If you are in a situation where it is not practical or possible to follow the above tip, try to relax yourself as much as you can. Do a Body Check and

release any muscles held unnecessarily tense, paying particular attention to your neck and shoulders. Then execute the Out-Breath Technique.

**6** If it is possible for you to lie down and rest, do so, but using either the technique for Lying stress-free and relaxed or the Total Relaxation with Mind-Clearing Technique. It will also help if you perform these techniques in the dark.

**7** I have also found the following visualizing technique remarkably effective in eliminating headaches. It is based on the premise that, if you wholly experience your pain, then the tension that you have been exerting to resist it will automatically diminish and your headache will subsequently go.

## HEADACHE CURE VISUALIZING TECHNIQUE

Sit or lie comfortably with your body and head well supported and your eyes closed. Mentally ask yourself and then answer the following three questions, in fairly rapid succession, allowing no more than a few seconds to consider your replies.

**Question 1** *Where is the pain?*
**Question 2** *How big is it?*
**Question 3** *What colour is it?*

Reply with whatever comes automatically into your mind and don't deliberate or let your mind wander. Concentrate completely.

The following is a typical example of how it works.

| QUESTION | ANSWER |
|---|---|
| Where is the pain? | Three inches down and four inches in, at the front, on the right side. |
| How big is it? | The size of an orange (plum, nut etc). |
| What colour is it? | Bright red (purple, black, white etc). |

You may have to repeat these questions to yourself over and over for several minutes and you may well find, that during this time the form, size and colour change.

# HYPERTENSION

Hypertension, or high blood pressure as it is commonly known, means that the heart is forced to work harder than it should in order to pump blood around the body. Hypertension was at one time thought to be solely due to medical reasons. Now it has been realized, however, that stress can both cause hypertension on its own and play a significant part in further aggravating the condition where it already exists.

It may be that your condition requires purely medical treatment. However, there are many cases of hypertension for which your doctor will also recommend that you learn how to relax. In these cases, you can safely follow the tips in this section. It is a good idea to actually show your doctor this book, however, so that he or she can familiarize themselves with the techniques and tell you whether or not they feel that they will be beneficial and appropriate to your particular case.

## WARNING

*I would stress that, since hypertension is such a potentially serious condition, self-diagnosis must never be attempted. If you feel, for any reason whatsoever, that you may be suffering from hypertension, I would most strongly urge you to seek immediate medical attention.*

## WHAT TO DO

Practise the following relaxation techniques regularly but not all in one go. Select one or two techniques to practise on any one day and then interchange them, so that in time you will do them all.

1 Out-Breath Technique (*see page 30*).

2 Natural Tranquillizing Technique (*see page 32*).

3 Sitting (*see page 36*).

4 Walking (*see page 38*).

5 Driving (*see page 40*).

6 Lying Down (*see page 42*).

7 Total Relaxation with Mind-Clearing Technique (*see page 46*).

8 Neck (*see page 52*).

9 Shoulders (*see page 56*).

10 Arms, Hands and Fingers (*see page 58*).

11 Legs and Feet (*see page 64*).

12 Body Check (*see page 66*).

# HYPERVENTILATION

Commonly known as 'overbreathing', hyperventilation is an excessive rate and depth of respiration which leads to an abnormal loss of carbon dioxide from the blood.

Anxiety is one of the chief causes of hyperventilation. What happens is that the breathing becomes quicker and more shallow and the heartbeat starts to race. Tightness is felt around the chest area, and a sense of panic sets in as it seems progressively more difficult to breathe. If the 'overbreathing' continues, the blood pressure can fall, due to the loss of carbon dioxide, resulting in the person fainting.

Hyperventilation can turn into a vicious circle inasmuch as, once it has been experienced, the fear and anxiety in case it happens again can be the cause of its recurrence. People who have a tendency to this faulty type of breathing sometimes suffer from acute panic attacks. If you are one of these people, practical advice on how to handle it is given later in this section (*see page 117*).

Since hyperventilation is often caused by tension and anxiety, the removal or reduction of these factors by learning how to relax will go a long way towards future prevention. The following tips contain the appropriate techniques for this. Specific breathing and relaxation techniques that can be applied when necessary to curtail an attack are also included.

A further technique given below is the very unorthodox-sounding 'Paper Bag Technique'. This remedy is very well-known and widely used for hyperventilation. It can rapidly restore the sufferer to normal by returning essential carbon dioxide to the lungs. As you will see, it entails nothing more complicated than breathing into a paper bag, but its effectiveness is well proven and you might like to try it.

## WHAT TO DO

1 Practise the following techniques regularly. Some will help to relax you generally and some, as you will see, are for when you are actually experiencing an attack.
- Out-Breath Technique (*see page 30*).
- Natural Tranquillizing Technique (*see page 32*).
- Deviation of Focus Technique (*see page 34*).
- Total Relaxation with Mind-Clearing Technique (*see page 46*).
- Deep Meditation (*see page 68*).
- Body Check (*see page 66*).

2 The moment you become aware that your breathing is quickening up, perform the Out-Breath Technique. Continue for several minutes until your breathing has slowed right down and you feel calm once more.

3 When your breathing quickens up, the body often tenses unconsciously too. Do a Body Check to see if this is the case, and let go of any muscles being held unnecessarily tense.

4 It sometimes happens, if you are prone to over-breathing, that without warning you suddenly become scared because you merely 'think' that you might have an attack, even before there have been any physical signs or reactions. If this occurs, immediately execute the Deviation of Focus Technique, concentrating completely on things outside yourself. Follow this up by executing the Out-Breath Technique a few times.

## THE PAPER BAG TECHNIQUE

5 If you find yourself unable to control your breathing at all and you are getting panicky, or find yourself going dizzy, simply hold a *small, thin* paper bag over your mouth and nose and breathe into it for a few minutes. Your breathing will then quickly return to normal. If you are prone to overbreathing and worry that it could happen to you at any time, then it is a good idea always to carry a paper bag with you in case of emergencies. This can often increase your confidence to such an extent that the attacks never occur again.

Another good reason for keeping a paper bag handy is so that you feel safe enough to try the previous tips first. Then, if they don't work, you know that you can fall back on the paper bag remedy. This will have a progressively relaxing effect, and you may find after a short time that your hyperventilation disappears altogether.

### WARNING
*Never use a plastic bag for this technique as it could adhere to your nose and mouth causing suffocation. Do not attempt to use on other people, either adults or children.*

---

The information given here should never be used as a substitute for seeing a doctor.

# INDIGESTION

Most of us suffer with indigestion from time to time, but tension and nervousness can greatly exacerbate this condition, making life very unpleasant. Indigestion can cause all manner of symptoms including heartburn, flatulence, nausea, distension of the stomach, loss of appetite and many others.

It is very important to relax whilst eating and there are techniques that will specifically help you to do this. There are also some important DO'S and DON'TS that should help to prevent indigestion occurring in the future.

## WHAT TO DO

1 Practise the following techniques regularly. They will not only help you to relax generally, but also be of great value when used at specific times to prevent indigestion.

- Out-Breath Technique (*see page 30*).
- Shoulders (*see page 56*).
- Stomach (*see page 60*).
- Body Check (*see page 66*).

2 Your body needs to be relaxed in order for your digestive system to work efficiently so get used to doing this little routine periodically whenever you are sitting and eating.

First, do a Body Check, and if you are holding any muscles unnecessarily tense, let them go, paying particular attention to your stomach and shoulder muscles. Then execute the Out-Breath Technique a few times.

3 Try to follow as many of these DO'S and DON'TS as you can.

## DO'S

- Do chew each mouthful well before swallowing.
- Do eat little and often rather than one huge meal at the end of the day.
- Do try to drink after your food rather than during meals where possible.
- Do sit comfortably, legs uncrossed, shoulders and stomach relaxed.
- Do really concentrate on your food, noticing how it looks, smells, tastes and so on.
- Do try to wait for a few minutes between each course.
- Do sit upright and relax for at least 20 minutes after you've eaten.

## DON'TS

- Don't rush your food if you can possibly help it.
- Don't eat rich or heavily spiced food.
- Don't talk at the same time as you eat.
- Don't go for long periods without eating.
- Don't eat too much at any one meal.
- Don't eat late at night.
- Don't eat foods that, from experience, don't agree with you.
- Don't consume fizzy drinks if you can avoid them.
- Don't sit crouched forward with your shoulders hunched.
- Don't immediately start to rush around or do anything energetic after a meal.
- Don't get engrossed in books, papers or television whilst eating.

# INSOMNIA

Very many people suffer from insomnia, which causes extreme stress, worry, anxiety and, of course, fatigue. The condition is one that feeds on itself because our worry and anxiety increase the likelihood of our continuing to suffer from it.

Insomnia not only makes us feel wretched and worn out, but it can also have much more serious medical implications. We are built in such a way that our bodies and our minds require a certain amount of rest in order to function properly. If we don't get it, the body becomes vulnerable to all sorts of diseases, infections and maladies, and the brain is unable to function efficiently.

Good quality sleep is essential for healthy living, and if you are an insomnia sufferer I suggest that you follow the advice and tips given in *Sleeping* (*see page 43*).

# MIGRAINE

Migraine can be one of the most crippling conditions experienced, and it is hard to imagine what it is like unless you have personally suffered from it.

It is definitely not just a bad headache, as is sometimes thought, even though it is easy to understand why non-sufferers might think this. It is true, however, that similar situations can sometimes precipitate both a headache and a migraine, but the symptoms are very different. These are some classic migraine symptoms:

Severe pain often located on only one side of the head.

Nausea, sometimes accompanied by vomiting.

Eyes becoming so ultra-sensitive to light that you simply have to shut them.

The sensation of seeing flashing lights or spots before the eyes.

Noises sounding amplified to an unbearable degree.

Not wanting to speak.

Loss of appetite.

Migraine is not one of those conditions that you can just 'grin and bear', hoping that as time goes on it will abate. You really do have to give in to it otherwise it normally gets very much worse.

Stress is known to be one of the main causes of migraine but it can also be triggered chemically, because of the body's intolerance to something in the diet. Cheese, chocolate, citrus fruit and red wine, for example, are commonly known to have this effect. It is often, therefore, very difficult to know whether it is stress or diet that is causing your migraine. If this is the case with you, I would recommend that you experiment by periodically omitting certain things from your diet. If you are fortunate enough to discover the 'trigger', you can then avoid it in the future.

## WHAT TO DO

**1** Practise in advance and familiarize yourself with the following techniques:

● Out-Breath Technique (*see page 30*).

● Total Relaxation with Mind-Clearing Technique (*see page 46*).

● Headache Cure Visualizing Technique (*see page 111*).

**2** As soon as you can, lie down in a quiet, darkened, cool room in the Total Relaxation Position. (It is fine to use either the bed or the floor).

**3** Loosen the clothing around your waist and neck. You may find that you need to use only one of the following tips in order to gain relief from your migraine, or all three tips used consecutively. Do whatever works best for you.

**4** Get comfortable and then perform the Out-Breath Technique, concentrating on feeling heavier and heavier with each exhalation. Simply continue until you feel calmer and more relaxed, or even go off to sleep.

**5** Execute the Total Relaxation with Mind-Clearing Technique, really concentrating on each part of the body and how it looks, as instructed.

**6** Execute the Headache Cure Visualizing Technique (*see page 111*).

**7** You might find it useful in terms of prevention to check through the list of some common causes of headache (*see page 111*), as often these causes can also apply to migraine attacks.

## MUSCLE PAIN

One of the most common reactions to stress is that we tense either specific muscle groups or sometimes the entire body, but we do this without realizing it. Often we keep these muscles tense and gripped for prolonged periods and this can result in muscle pain. This pain can range in severity from mild to acute, especially where the neck, back and shoulder muscles are concerned.

We need to be able to 'tune in ' to our muscles, so that we can easily recognize when they are in a tense state and when they are in a relaxed state. Then, when we find ourselves in a stressful situation, we can instantly let them go. This physical release also brings about automatic removal of the stress, and relaxation is the result.

### *WHAT TO DO*

**I** Stress Cure A contains specific cures giving advice and tips on how to instantly relax the various parts of the body that commonly tense up when we become stressed (*see pages 48 to 66*).

Read and practise the techniques that apply to your particular problem.

**2** Also practise the Body Check (*see page 66*), as this will enable you to do quick checks, no matter where you are or what you are doing, to locate the muscle tension and to release it immediately.

## NAIL-BITING AND SIMILAR HABITS

Although nail-biting is one of the most common 'nervous' habits among people who suffer from stress and anxiety, there are a number of other such habits of which the following are a few:

Picking at the nails or surrounding skin
Constantly touching or scratching the face
Fiddling with the hair
Constantly picking the fluff off one's clothes
Constantly drumming the fingers.
These habits don't necessarily cause any physical harm, but they are a very good indication that we are nervous, tense and stressed. We need, therefore, to be able to read these habits as stress signals so that we can

immediately do something about relaxing and letting go.

They can also cause embarrassment, because often the people that are afflicted by them try unsuccessfully to hide them from others, knowing that the habit may reveal how nervous and anxious they really are.

If you are suffering from any of the above, or similar, habits and would like to try to stop, these tips should help you.

### *WHAT TO DO*

**I** Practise the following techniques regularly so that they are familiar to you.

● Out-Breath Technique (*see page 30*).

- Sitting (*see page 36*).
- Arms, Hands and Fingers (*see page 58*).
- Body Check (*see page 66*).

**2** The moment you catch yourself biting your nails, repeatedly scratching or touching your face, or whatever, do a Body Check. When you come to the arms and hands, consciously change their position, putting them somewhere where they can totally relax.

**3** You will probably find that you want to repeat your habit a few moments later. Counteract this as soon as you feel the urge by leaving the hands in a relaxed position and executing the Out-Breath Technique.

**4** We often indulge in these sorts of habits when we are sitting down. If this applies to you, follow the instructions given under *Sitting*, paying particular attention to the arm and hand positions.

**5** These habits can be broken, but you need to get used to how it feels when your arms and hands are totally relaxed and when they are tense. You will do this by practising the Arms, Hands and Fingers Technique.

**6** No matter how long you have been suffering with your particular habit, you have the power to stop it. However, you do have to make a concerted effort to keep correcting your hand and arm positions so that they can relax. It may not happen overnight but persevere, because if you apply the cures you have a very good chance of being totally successful.

# PANIC ATTACKS

These extremely frightening attacks are suffered by many people and are brought on by anxiety, tension, nervousness and stress. Panic attacks can happen no matter where you are or what you are doing, and can have a severely restricting effect on your life. Many people, for example, experience them whilst out in public places which can then make them reluctant to go out again. Others may be prone to them when in a crowd and, as a result, they will avoid crowded places. Then there are those who avoid lifts, aeroplanes, and all sorts of other situations for the same reasons. Phobias can often be the result of these avoidance tactics. Panic attacks also happen to people who are alone in their own homes. They can be absolutely petrified in case something terrible should happen to them.

## Let's Look at What a Panic Attack is

A panic attack is when you suddenly tense up and, in so doing, restrict your breathing to the extent that you feel drastically short of breath.

This leads to you gasping for air and feeling heavy and tight around the chest. Your heart begins to race and you may also start to get extremely hot and sweaty and to think that you are going to faint or even die.

The most important thing for you to know if you suffer from panic attacks is that, in spite of how it may feel, *a panic attack won't actually do you any harm.* Keep telling yourself that fact, because it is often the fear alone of what might happen that brings on the attack.

Another important thing for you to remember is that you and only you have created this panic attack. Nothing and nobody outside yourself has the power to do this. In the same way, it is you who can reverse the process, undo what is happening, and put a stop to the attack.

***Note:*** See also *Stress and How it Affects the Whole of You* (*page 15*) and *Hyperventilation* (*page 112*).

## WHAT TO DO

**1** It is very important to learn and regularly practise the following techniques because you will need them to ward off your next attack.

- Out-Breath Technique (*see page 30*).
- Deviation of Focus Technique (*see page 34*).
- Body Check (*see page 66*).

**2** The moment you become aware of the panic building inside you, begin the Deviation of Focus Technique, concentrating totally on things outside yourself. Continue with this technique for a minimum of three minutes.

**3** After performing the above, do the Out-Breath Technique and continue for several minutes until you feel considerably calmer and your breathing has slowed down.

**Note:** *If you are able to, sit down at this stage as this will help you to relax. The technique, however, will still work if done standing up.*

**4** Lastly, do a Body Check to see which muscles you are gripping unnecessarily and let them go. Then return to the Out-Breath Technique for a few more minutes.

## PRE-MENSTRUAL TENSION

Pre-menstrual tension, or PMT as it is commonly known, is suffered by many women every single month for several days before the start of each period. It can cause, among other things, depression, irritability, fatigue, sensitive and painful breasts, headache or migraine, dizziness and a feeling of being bloated.

In the past, the medical profession tended to label this 'neurotic' but now it is widely accepted that PMT can be an extremely distressing problem. Some women suffer so badly that their only way of coping is to 'opt out' of life until the PMT has passed, knowing that they will probably feel the same again next month. Others report dramatic character changes leading to strange and unaccustomed behaviour. It is a statistical fact that women are more prone to commit minor offences, such as shop-lifting, at this time, and occasionally even violent crime.

If you suffer from PMT, then stress can contribute greatly to your condition. Learning to remove stress via relaxation can therefore make a considerable difference. The tips given here contain specific relaxation techniques and some important do's and don'ts that should help to ease, reduce or even eliminate your PMT.

## WHAT TO DO

**1** Practise these relaxation techniques regularly:
- Total Relaxation with Mind-Clearing Technique (*see page 46*).
- Deep Meditation (*see page 68*).
- Body Check (*see page 66*).

**2** During, and for a few days before, the onset of PMT try to apply as many of these *Do's* and *Don'ts* as you can.

## DO'S

- Do make a point of practising either the Total Relaxation with Mind-Clearing Technique or the Deep Meditation technique every day.
- Do cut down your salt intake a little, because there is a tendency towards water retention which causes bloatedness.
- Do try to get some extra rest for yourself.
- Do use the Body Check whenever you are feeling tense, to release the relevant muscle groups.

## DON'TS

- Don't eat or drink heavily.
- Don't do anything too strenuous.
- Don't rush around.
- Don't begin new or demanding projects.
- Don't allow yourself to get into heated discussions or arguments if you can possibly help it.
- Don't go into hot, overcrowded, noisy rooms if you can possibly avoid it.

# SKIN CONDITIONS

There are many skin conditions that can be influenced and made much worse by the presence of anxiety and stress. If you aren't sure whether your condition comes into this category, check with your doctor. If he confirms that stress is a relevant factor, you may find both relief and improvement by doing the following relaxation techniques.

## WHAT TO DO

1 Total Relaxation with Mind-Clearing Technique (*see page 46*).
2 Deep Meditation (*see page 68*).

# STUTTERING

Stuttering can be caused or greatly exacerbated by anxiety, nervousness and stress. Unfortunately the embarrassment and shame felt when other people notice this speech impediment adds to the stutterer's distress.

Learning how to relax with the aid of various techniques can go a long way towards the alleviation of this condition.

Good breath control and the ability to breathe deeply make a significant difference to the reduction or complete cessation of stuttering, and the techniques below should be learnt and practised.

## WHAT TO DO

1 Practise the following techniques regularly. Some will help you to relax generally and others will help you when you find yourself stuttering.

• Out-Breath Technique (*see page 30*).
• Deviation of Focus Technique (*see page 34*).
• Total Relaxation with Mind-Clearing Technique (*see page 46*).
• Face (*see page 50*).
• Body Check (*see page 66*).

2 When you find yourself stuttering, first do a Body Check. Notice which muscles you are holding unnecessarily tense and let them go.
3 Next, concentrate on the Out-Breath Technique for a few moments.
4 You are now ready to take a deep, smooth breath. Then wait for a second or two, before you speak, as calmly as you can. Do this every time you speak.
5 If you find after several attempts that you simply can't stop stuttering, try the Deviation of Focus Technique for a few moments, concentrating completely on things outside yourself, exactly as instructed. Then try again, taking the pre-requisite deep breath.
6 Don't be deterred by thinking that the tips given above will take a long time to follow. In reality, they will only take you a few moments, and unless the person you are talking to is unusually impatient, he or she will willingly wait.

## SWEATING (EXCESSIVE)

There are many people who perspire profusely when they become anxious and tense. This can, of course, cause embarrassment, which in turn creates more anxiety and tension.

The following techniques and tactics will help you literally to cool down and relax, and can be a great help.

### *WHAT TO DO*
**1** Practise the Total Relaxation with Mind-Clearing Technique on a regular basis. (Daily or on alternate days, for example, *see page 46*).

**2** Practise the Out-Breath Technique and the Body Check until they are very familiar because you will need them for 'on the spot' help.

**3** When you become aware of yourself getting hot, do a Body Check, altering your position if necessary, so that you can release any muscles that are being held tense. If it is convenient, sit down.

**4** Then practise the Out-Breath Technique, concentrating on the slowness of the breath, as instructed. Continue this for several minutes until you feel cooler and more relaxed.